Child Abuse in the Deep South

T0307936

Institute for Social Science Research
Monograph Series

General Editor, Philip B. Coulter

*Political Voice: Citizen Demand for Urban
Public Services,* by Philip B. Coulter

*Child Abuse in the Deep South: Geographical
Modifiers of Abuse Characteristics,* by Lee W. Badger,
Nicholas A. Green, L. Ralph Jones, and Julia A. Hartman

Child Abuse in the Deep South

Geographical Modifiers of Abuse Characteristics

Lee W. Badger
Nicholas A. Green
L. Ralph Jones
Julia A. Hartman

Published for the
Institute for Social Science Research by
The University of Alabama Press   *Tuscaloosa*

The University of Alabama Press
Tuscaloosa, Alabama 35487-0380
uapress.ua.edu

Typeface: Times

Manufactured in the United States of America
Cover design: Paula Dennis

∞
The paper on which this book is printed meets the minimum requirements of
American National Standard for Information Science–Permanence of Paper for
Printed Library Materials, ANSI Z39.48-1984.

Paperback ISBN: 978-0-8173-0363-1
eBook ISBN: 978-0-8173-8985-7

A previous edition of this book has been catalogued by the Library of Congress
as follows:

Library of Congress Cataloging-in-Publication Data
  Child abuse in the Deep South.
  (ISSR monograph series ; no. 2)
  Bibliography : p.
  Includes index.
  1. Child abuse—Alabama.   2. Alabama—Rural conditions.   3. City and town
life—Alabama.
  I. Badger, Lee W., 1943–   .   II. University of Alabama. Institute of Social
Science Research. III. Series. [DNLM: 1. Child Abuse. 2. Rural Population—
Alabama. 3. Urban Population— Alabama. WA   320   C53418]
HV6626.5.C495   1988   362.7'044   86–30891
ISBN 0-8173-0363-4

British Library Cataloguing-in-Publication Data is available.

Contents

Tables

Figures

Preface

This study evolved, as is true of many, from a question unanswered in the existing literature. At the start, we wanted to know whether child abuse was more prevalent in rural areas or in the cities. Not surprisingly, two of us had firm—and opposing—opinions. Interest grew, and in the fall of 1983 we met in Montgomery with Ms. Mary Carswell, the Director of Protective Services of the Department of Pensions and Security (DPS), to discuss a project designed to answer the question. The discussion raised many additional and important questions about child abuse and it was clear that the DPS Central Registry was the place to look for the answers. This monograph is the result of that investigation. We are grateful for the cooperation and support we received from the former Commissioner of DPS, Dr. Leon Frazier, from Ms. Louise Pittman, the Director of the Bureau of Family and Children Services, and, of course, from Ms. Carswell and the entire (and tireless) Protective Services staff. We are also indebted to the anonymous reviewers who made helpful comments on an earlier version of this manuscript.

We thank Ms. Gloria Keller who typed (and retyped) the manuscript with a patience and good humor that lasted through to the final product.

L. W. B.

PART ONE
Historical Perspectives and Current Understandings

1
The Problem of Definitions

A major handicap to the value of all research findings has been the lack of consistent and nonoverlapping definitions of child abuse. Mental health professionals are therapeutically oriented and focus on families; medical professionals are physically oriented and focus on the injuries to the victim; legal authorities are oriented toward conviction and focus on the perpetrator; and the general public is anxiously oriented toward its own welfare and safety. In "The Battered-Child Syndrome," Kempe et al. (1962), for example, described a clinical condition with diagnosable medical and physical symptoms. Shortly thereafter, Fontana, Donovan, and Wong (1963) described the "maltreatment syndrome," which included children without obvious physical signs of battering but with evidence of emotional and nutritional deprivation, neglect, and abuse. Gil's (1970) definition, based on his large-scale study of child abuse incidence, was broader and more socially oriented, ultimately including abuse not only by caretakers but also by institutions and society at large. Policies that sanctioned or failed to overcome deficits in the circumstances of children were thus implicated. Elmer (1966) asserted that the chronicity of abuse was also an important variable in definition, and she proposed that social class and ethnicity be entered into the clinical definition of child abuse. A most useful definition of a physically abused child, provided by Kempe and Helfer in 1972, was "any child who receives nonaccidental physical injury (or injuries) as a result of acts (or omissions) on the part of his parents or guardians" (p. xi). Obvious difficulties still remain nonetheless: for example, how does one prove "nonaccidental," and what about injury inflicted by an adult other than a parent or guardian?

The result of these variations in definition is that abuse is, in fact, defined by those instances in which victimization becomes publicly known and labeled by an official or professional. Gelles (1975) called this the social construction of abuse, in which certain judges or gatekeepers apply the labels of "abuse" and "abuser" to particular individuals and families. Korbin (1981) noted also that child-rearing practices vary between cultures: what is acceptable behavior in one group may be totally unacceptable behavior in another.

In sexual abuse, this problem has even greater implications, especially for the value of research findings as a means to tailor treatment to the specific underlying pathology. Over the last ten years, different terms have been used for the same type of sexual offense, and concepts have been intermixed and overgeneralized to include every type of reported event under the general term "sexual abuse." At this juncture, epidemiological research of child sexual abuse cannot measure the degree of change in the rates of incidence and prevalence because definitions have changed from one period to another. It is important that legal authorities, legislators, medical and social service professionals, researchers, and the public standardize the definitions of child sexual abuse for the benefit of all.

Most state laws and agencies today include the following components in their definitions of child sexual abuse: (1) sexual contacts or interactions of any sort between a child and an adult (or significantly older person) whether the sexual contact was instigated by the adult or the child (some definitions make reference to a minimum age differential between perpetrator and child, so that it is conceivable that an older child could be charged with "sexual abuse" of a younger child; the inference, of course, is that the older child is in a position of power or control over the victim); (2) the use or exploitation of a child for the sexual stimulation of an adult or another person; (3) a "child" is defined as anyone under a legal age of consent, which in most states is sixteen to eighteen years of age. Any child or adolescent under the designated age of consent is by definition "unable to give informed consent" for any sexual act or behavior. It is interesting that many states set the age of consent for child sexual abuse statutes at an older age than that established for marriage.

Sexual abuse, as mentioned above, is a catchall term that includes a number of categories referred to in the literature and incorporated within legal definitions but that often have different meanings attached. For example, the term sexual misuse has been defined by some states and agencies to include sexual stimulation inappropriate for the age and development of the child, including acts such as allowing a child to see pornographic films. Other writers have used it synonymously with sexual exploitation and with sexual abuse generally.

Sexual molestation, a vague, ill-defined term that is often used synonymously with "taking indecent liberties," implies a range of physical contacts from kissing and seductive touching to masturbation. Usually, however, it does not involve sexual intercourse or sodomy. Sexual molestation has been given more explicit legal definition in some court jurisdictions to delineate a degree of sexual abuse less than rape, and it is sometimes used as an alternative charge when a conviction on an incest charge does not appear possible. In other contexts, sexual molestation is used as a term descriptive of a type of incestuous activity.

Rape is often defined to include sodomy and oral-genital sexual contacts, although there are some localities that restrict their definition to the older concept of vaginal penetration only. Digital penetration is included within some definitions of rape, and homosexual activities with children have, therefore, been included under this definition. Rape of children, whether it be forcible or statutory, is frequently labeled "sexual assault" in public records. This practice seriously limits the distinction of those factors relevant to seductive rape from those pertaining to aggressive rape. It has been suggested that the use of the term "sexual assault" be restricted to imply some degree of violence or threat of violence, to contrast with the term "sexual seduction," involving intercourse, which has an entirely different set of dynamics and effects.

Incestuous sexual abuse indicates sexual violation of the cultural taboos of family roles and, in the past, was defined as overt sexual intercourse occurring between "blood relations." This definition has changed, in most jurisdictions, to include sexual molestation of any sort among any members of a family group who are not permitted by their society to marry. Therefore, incest includes sexual molestation by stepfathers and stepsiblings, an appropriate inclusion when current morality and sexual practices are considered. The most common form of incest occurs between siblings and stepsiblings or cousins but, because of the minimal age differential in most instances, is not included under the definition of sexual abuse. The most commonly reported incidents involve father-daughter and stepfather-stepdaughter incest. Incestuous sexual abuse does not usually involve violent assault, and it sometimes offers gratification for the victim, often without significant anxiety or physical suffering; it tends to be recurrent and progressive with a chronic course.

Pedophilia was originally defined as an erotic preference for immature sexual gratification with a prepubertal child (Mohr, Turner, and Jerry, 1964). Many child abuse laws have broadened the usage to include offenses with adolescent victims. The term pedophilia has, at times in the past, erroneously been used as a synonym for child sexual abuse, but only about 20 percent of child sexual abuse has technically fallen within the current definition of pedophilia. Because they are attracted to more immature levels of sexuality, most fixated pedophiliacs do not commit forcible rape and are usually charged with "sexual molestation" as defined above. Some pedophiliacs molest their own children and fall under a special class of "incestuous pedophilia," although most pedophiliacs are not incestuous. Another subgroup is homosexual pedophilia known as pederasty.

Exhibitionism, or indecent exposure, is the most frequently documented sex crime against children. Offenders are primarily male, and most exhibitionists make no attempt to touch a child but are content to elicit an effective response of alarm from a victim. Cases that have been included under the definitions of exhibitionism range from drunks urinating in public, to classical benign exhibitionism, to solicitations, to those rare instances that are preludes to seduction. Exhibitionism's broad scope renders it one of the most frequent contaminators of statistical data on perpetrators of sexual abuse. Because not all recorded incidents of exhibition, as loosely defined, constitute true sexual abuse, a need is clearly indicated for refinement of this category.

Sexual exploitation, as defined by Alabama law and elsewhere, includes "allowing, permitting, or encouraging a child to engage in prostitution" and "allowing, permitting, encouraging or engaging in the obscene or pornographic photography, filming, or depicting of a child for commercial purposes."

Whereas legal authorities have attempted to categorize abusive sexual behaviors in terms of degree of violence and associated inherent dangers, epidemiological researchers have been inclined to categorize sexual abuse in a manner that emphasizes demographic data and the relationship of the perpetrator to the child, the most common dichotomy being "familial" (or "intrafamilial" or "incestuous") and "extrafamilial" (or "nonfamilial") sexual abuse. Another distinction is made between recurrent (or chronic) abuse and single event (or acute) abuse. For example, most incestuous abuse tends to be chronic, and most extrafamilial sexual abuse is a single event.

Refinements of these definitions of sexual abuse should consider effects upon the victim and the implicit differences in the etiology, management, and treatment of the various forms that abuse takes. A clinical orientation to a classification of child sexual abuse should take into account the psychological impact upon the child, including the acute and chronic consequences, as well as the adult sequelae of sexual abuse. It is generally accepted that single events of sexual abuse have milder and fewer long-term effects upon the child than recurrent sexual abuse. Sexual abuse has more deleterious and complex long-term effects when the sexual experience is invasive of the child's development (in terms of the victim's age, phases of development, and inherent relationship to the perpetrator) and when the abuse is more symptomatic of family pathology. For example, the predominant consequences of parent-child incest result from the cumulative effects of disrupted psychosexual development of the child, disturbances in family role-imaging, and in the failure to define the boundaries of relationships and the limits of acceptable sexual behavior necessary for learning to control sexual impulses. Confusion of erotic love with parental affection occurs, as does undermining of trust and self-image of both the child and the spouse.

Short-term effects of incestuous sexual abuse include regression to infantile habits and behaviors, eating and sleep disorders, enuresis, and conduct disorders, especially dysinhibition of sexual impulses and the seeking of affection through sexual contact. Later sequels include runaway behavior, promiscuity, prostitution, pornographic exploitation, substance abuse, and other forms of antisocial behavior. There is some indication that older children suffer more serious long-term effects than younger children (Finkelhor, 1979). There is a predisposition to guilt, demoralization, and depression; suicide gestures and self-mutilation are also believed to have a high incidence among this group. As adults, victims of incest are more prone to having difficulties in forming intimate trusting relationships, often fail to marry, and have a higher incidence of sexual dysfunctions. Finally, there is the increased likelihood that the childhood victims of parent incest will become the next generation of perpetrators.

Parent-child incest usually occurs in the context of a disturbed family setting, which has other effects upon the child in addition to those that are specific for sexual abuse. The general theme of disturbances within the family dynamics includes a closed-family system with an alien view of the outside world and the misrepresentation of moral standards, a paradoxical lack of limits within the context of overcontrol by the dominant perpetrator, blurring of role boundaries, the lack of nurturing relationships, and marital discord. Child pornography and prostitution are related in that both are frequent sequels to chronic incestuous sexual abuse. Bagley (1984) reported that 30 percent of the girls in the study sample who later became prostitutes had their first sexual experience with a family member or someone in a position of trust. Sixty-three percent of a sample of young female prostitutes and 77 percent of male prostitutes were found to be fully sexually experienced by the age of thirteen. Further findings suggested that the decision to enter into prostitution was not voluntary but reflected the coercion of poverty and homelessness associated with attempts on the part of juveniles to escape abusive situations at home. More than two-thirds of these youngsters had a history of running away from home prior to engaging in prostitution (Bagley, 1984).

Another important factor affecting the impact upon the child, or the degree of victim-registered abuse, is the response and the interpretation of the event by significant adults in the child's life. A calm, objective, supportive parent offering timely and appropriate responses can turn a potentially anxious or guilt-laden event into a relatively innocuous experience that results in none of the anticipated "abusive" effects.

The following proposed classification takes into account the etiology of abuse as well as the effects of sexual abuse on the victim and the important differences in management and treatment.

1. Sexual assault: This category includes forcible rape, battered injuries to genital area, and sexual molestation that involves physical contact and some form of violence or threat of violence.

2. Sexual seduction: This category includes the enticement of the child to willingly participate in a progression of sexual behavior through the use of deceptive inducements, bribes, ego enhancements, or subtle coercion without threat of violent force, coupled with implicit sanctioning of the behavior by a familiar authority figure:
   a. Familial seduction, or incest
   b. Extrafamilial seduction, or pedophilia.

3. Sexual exposure: This category includes nontactile sexual experiences, including exhibitionism, solicitations, and obscenities.

4. Sexual exploitation: This category includes commercial exploitation, including prostitution and pornography.

The problems of inconsistency in definition in the literature and other historical reports and documents preclude a scientific comparison of the incidence of sexual abuse in the past time periods with today. Therefore, no definitive conclusion can be made as to whether sexual abuse is on the rise or on the decline (Franklin, 1984). Thus we are left only to speculate at this point. But perhaps we should be mindful of the warning of Margaret Mead (1968) that the incidence of incest in a society may be a more valid measure of the disruption of the sociocultural system than the usual indexes of suicide, homocide, and crime.

2
Physical Child Abuse

Throughout history, the role assigned to children has reflected prevailing social and moral values. Until the widespread reforms of the nineteenth century, many types of abuse to children (according to today's definition) were not only generally accepted but were formally sanctioned—by religious bodies, by common law and written statute, or simply by community tradition. During early Roman times, children were the chattel of their father and dependent upon his decision as to whether they should live or die. Infanticide was commonly practiced, even after its formal opposition by the Roman Catholic church in the fourth century. During the Protestant Reformation, religious doctrine emphasized the importance of a parent's responsibility to rid children of their innate wickedness, making whippings both common and acceptable. During the eighteenth century, these beliefs were challenged by the writings of philosophers such as Rousseau and Locke, who emphasized that children were innately innocent and susceptible to social corruption. It therefore evolved upon society to assume responsibility for those children whose moral and ethical education was not properly supervised by their parents. Community interest was not focused on the child, however, but on the protection of the society's overall economic welfare and moral values. In the United States, for example, townships established formal mechanisms for the surveillance of all families, especially if they were poor, and for the necessary removal of children whose moral upbringing was questioned.

In the United States during the early nineteenth century, specialized institutions, such as orphanages and reformatories, were founded for these children by private charitable organizations, guided by principles borrowed from the English poor laws. The purpose of these institutions was to provide asylum for children from the malevolence and poverty of their parents, and the right to remove children from their parents' custody went virtually unchallenged until midcentury. In 1838 the legality of the involuntary placement of a child in a reformatory was challenged and upheld on the basis of the doctrine of *parens patriae*. This principle, established in early Christian doctrine and continuing to present day, defined the authority of a state to intervene in matters pertaining to a family. Over the next half century, thousands of destitute children were removed, mostly without judicial review, and even transferred thousands of miles away from their families.

The latter part of the nineteenth century was a period of heightened activity and influence among social reformers. Central to their message was that destitution was not synonymous with questionable moral character and that families should, therefore, not be dissolved by reason of poverty alone. Public notoriety surrounding the case of a New York child routinely beaten by her stepmother prompted the founding, in 1874, of the Society for the Prevention of Cruelty to Children (SPCC), the first organized attempt to protect, not poor, but mistreated children. Three years later, the American Humane Society (AHS) was founded as a national umbrella organization for the many societies that grew out of New York's example. Although the early SPCCs and the AHS served as an investigative arm of the courts, over the decades their philosophy and their manner became more therapeutic than punitive, reflecting more of a social work orientation.

The gradual adoption of specialty courts for juveniles, beginning in Illinois in 1899, reflected growing sentiment that, in judicial matters, children should be neither defined nor treated as adults or as criminals. Reevaluation of a family's rights with respect to its children, a major emphasis of the social reform movement, was the focus of the first White House Conference on Children, called by President Theodore Roosevelt in 1909. The conference resulted both in the formal establishment of the Children's Bureau in the Department of Labor and in a national ideological commitment to the preservation of the family. Although it was recognized that maintenance and support of poor families required financial assistance from the federal government, not until three decades later, in 1935, was such support legislated with the passage of the Social Security Act. The act provided funding for "the protection and care of homeless, dependent and neglected children and children in danger of becoming delinquent." The development of child protective services within state departments of welfare rapidly followed the allocation of this earmarked federal funding.

In spite of these initiatives from both the private and the public sectors, the general public remained essentially ignorant and indifferent to child maltreatment. Public concern evolved very gradually, as did interest within the medical community.

The first medical recognition of unacceptable treatment of children came in the form of an article written by Ambroise Tardieu in 1860 that reported the unexplained deaths of thirty-two children (Silverman, 1972). Although a few similar articles were published over the next half century, prior to an article published by Silverman in 1953 no physician dared more than to suggest that some mysterious injuries might have been willfully inflicted by the child's parents. In 1962, during a time of widespread human and civil rights advocacy, Kempe, Silverman, Steele, Droegmueller, and Silver wrote an article with the purposefully sensational title of "The Battered-Child Syndrome." The article, published in the *Journal of the American Medical Association,* described radiologic evidence of the mistreatment of children, which had previously been thought untenable. Today that article is generally accepted as a catalyst for the important legislative actions of the 1960s and 1970s. By 1965, every state had enacted a child abuse reporting law modeled after the version drafted by the United States Children's Bureau.

Over the next decade, the U.S. Senate Subcommittee on Children and Youth held a series of hearings that resulted, in 1974, in the passage of Public Law 93–247, also known as the Mondale Act or, more descriptively, as the National Child Abuse Prevention and Treatment Act. The act created the National Center on Child Abuse and Neglect as a support mechanism for the states. Subsequently, the center contracted for the first national study of the incidence and severity of child abuse and neglect.

Current Understandings

The recognition of child abuse as a significant social and public health problem and the documentation required by mandatory reporting laws made possible the epidemiological investigation into various risk factors associated with child abuse. The literature devoted to child abuse over the past two decades reveals a dramatic increase in interest by researchers and clinicians. There is now an increased awareness of the importance of differentiating between the forms that abuse takes and their differential incidence in population subgroups. Physical and sexual abuse are understood to result from multidimensional and unique networks of personal, social, and environmental factors and should, therefore, be independently explored (Jason, Williams, Burton, and Rochat, 1982).

Although an unknown number of abused children escape detection, nationally about one million annual reports are made of abused and neglected children (American Medical Association Council on Scientific Affairs, 1985). Only reported abuse can be investigated epidemiologically, and it provides clues both to the nature of child abuse and to the social and cultural factors that contribute to reporting.

Nonetheless, interpretation of research findings, some of which are briefly reviewed below, must attend to the reality that hypothesized risk factors may become confounded with artifactual factors resulting from selective reporting. In a 1982 study of this problem, Jason, Andereck, Marks, and Tyler compared founded and ruled-out reports of child abuse from the computerized central registry in Georgia and confirmed that several perpetrator and victim categories were inflated due to heightened surveillance or reporting. Newberger and Hyde (1975) also found that hospital reports of child abuse identified more low socioeconomic families due to their greater use of emergency rooms and to the tendency of hospitals to diagnose injuries as accidental when they occur in higher income families.

Reporting may, therefore, contribute to an exaggerated *proportion* of cases associated with a particular variable, but it usually cannot completely explain away the association. For example, many studies have shown that poverty, as measured by actual income, unemployment, or a history of welfare, is a factor associated with child abuse (AHS, 1978; Gil, 1969; Pelton, 1978), yet this finding is often rebutted by the argument that it is produced by the overreporting of poverty families and not by a true high incidence of abuse among them. Pelton (1978), however, has argued well that "both evidence and reason lead to the unmistakable conclusion that, contrary to the myth of classlessness, child abuse and neglect are strongly related to poverty" (p. 616). Support of this position was provided by Jason, Andereck, Marks, and Tyler (1982), who found that families who had received Aid to Dependent Children were in fact at risk of abuse rather than only at risk of being reported. Daniel, Hampton, and Newberger (1983) concluded from their study, using a matched control group design, that "the prevalence of poverty in the families of abuse victims is one of the striking demographic findings" (p. 649). These studies do not deny that abuse may take place in families that are not poor; they do, however, confirm that poverty is a factor in a large number of the cases of abuse.

White children have been found to be more often abused in two-parent families (Jason, Williams, Burton, and Rochat, 1982; McCarthy et al., 1981), while black children have been found to be at greater risk in families headed by a woman (Gil, 1969; McCarthy et al., 1981). Female-headed households are often poor, confounding the effects of poverty and family type. Risk assessment is also complicated by the fact that in some parts of the country female-headed households represent the modal living arrangement for black children and are, therefore, the expected household type in any characterization of black families.

Characteristics of perpetrators have also been explored in child abuse epidemiology. It has been reported that perpetrators tend to be young (Baldwin and Oliver, 1975; Lauer, Ten Broeck, and Grossman, 1974) and that mothers are the most frequent abusers (Steele and Pollock, 1974). Overreporting of poor parents, however, would lower the average age of the perpetrator, due to their generally younger age of marriage and parturition, and consequently lower the average age of the abused child as well. In fact, the finding that younger children are at greater risk (Gil,

1970; Jason and Andereck, 1983; Hampton and Newberger, 1985)
was considered a condition associated only with greater surveillance in the analysis reported by Jason, Andereck, Marks, and
Tyler (1982).

Current theories of child abuse etiology incorporate the inter-
action of psychological dimensions along with the social and environmental components. For example, Kempe and Steele have
identified three ingredients necessary for abuse to occur: a child
who is seen as "bad" or different, potentially abusive parents,
and stress (Weissberg, 1983). The latter, stress, is thought to result
from relationship difficulties, job demands, or social isolation
(Gelles, 1973, 1980; Gil, 1970; Parke and Collmer, 1975; Straus,
Gelles, and Steinmetz, 1980). A cycle of violence is thought to be
a response to stress that is learned from exposure to violence as a
child and that leads to the multigenerational nature of child abuse
(Parke and Collmer, 1975; Weissberg, 1983).

The Alabama Study

Overall, as has been shown, the contribution of specific demographic characteristics to the incidence of abuse remains equivocal (Department of Health, Education, and Welfare, 1977). This
study was guided by the premise that the importance of epidemiological research in child abuse lies less in its capacity to
quantify specific risk factors associated with abusers or victims
than in its capacity to identify the broader social systems or contexts in which abuse occurs. As O'Brien (1971) concluded: "The
family, as a social system, functions in close dynamic analog to
that of the society at large. . . . [Violent behavior, such as child
abuse, may represent] the family centered venting of the ag-
gressiveness . . . which had its antecedents in frustrations en-
countered in the larger structures of the social and economic
world" (p. 696).

Greater efficacy and precision in service delivery can result
only after the identification of the kinds of communities in which
child abuse is a problem. Once such community types are known,
the next step is to explore whether a discovered high prevalence is

due to greater risk for abuse or, conversely, whether it reflects a surveillance-reporting system working effectively. Without identified populations, treatment must remain nonspecific and random, and there can be little expectation of effective intervention.

Few studies, however, have included measures of cultural context; studies that have looked at the type of community in which abuse occurs have used a rural/urban dichotomy defined by the Standard Metropolitan Statistical Area (SMSA). The SMSA is a statistical standard developed for use by federal agencies in the production, analysis, and publication of data on metropolitan areas, as defined by the U.S. Office of Management and Budget. Each SMSA has one or more central counties containing the area's main population concentration, an urbanized area with at least 50,000 inhabitants. This population is usually referred to as a metropolitan population. Seven SMSA counties were in the study sample. Although SMSA designations are useful for many governmental functions, they are based upon the county unit, which necessarily includes not only the urban population but persons living in remote rural regions of the county as well. As a result, use of the SMSA is misleading when trying to sort out the socioeconomic, or even geographic, factors in urban and rural living with the occurrence of child abuse.

The population of Alabama is largely rural; more than half (52.3 percent) of the state's white residents and 38.8 percent of the state's black residents live in rural areas of fewer than 10,000 inhabitants. Towns and small cities, on the other hand, have populations of between 10,000 and 50,000 and do not geographically fringe any large metropolitan center. Fewer than 6 percent of Alabama's residents live in these communities. The third community type, the urbanized area, is composed of an incorporated place and adjacent densely settled surrounding area that together have a minimum population of 50,000. Fifty-five percent of Alabama's black population and 42 percent of Alabama's white population live in urbanized areas.

One would expect these community differences to contribute to a unique picture of surveillance, reporting, and caseworker determination of abuse. This descriptive analysis of child abuse in the

state of Alabama was conducted in order to investigate the hypothesized influence of cultural context as reflected by community
size. While also attending to the same variables that have inter-
ested other researchers, this study analyzed the variety and frequency of reporting sources as indicators of the level of vigilance
and support within Alabama's rural, midsized, and urbanized
areas.

3
Sexual Child Abuse

Sexual abuse of children, and particularly incestuous abuse, has always been a controversial issue. Until the 1960s, there had been a tendency to avoid acknowledging its existence as a significant social problem and a consequent lack of systematic studies of the subject. Factors contributing to this avoidance have been numerous. Generally, authors have referred to the long-standing repressive attitude toward sexuality stemming to the Victorian era and, particularly, the tendency to deny childhood sexuality. Society's disgust, aversion, and anxiety associated with the confrontation of sexual child abuse have perpetrated myths that have served to rationalize and minimize concerns among the middle class, such as the belief that incest is rare and occurs primarily among the primitive poor and the insane. Furthermore, the recognition of sexual child abuse has been inherently dependent upon its definition. The definition of sexual abuse has been varied and inconsistent, as has been the definition of childhood itself. To extricate our thinking from the prejudicial influences of the past, it is important to evaluate the history of sexual treatment of children.

The Historical Rationalization

Up to the sixteenth century, secular law in Western society reflected no interest in prohibiting child-adult sexual practices. In spite of early Christian attempts to preserve the rights of children, the taboo against the sexual use of children by adults has been with us for only a few hundred years. Indeed, until the seventeenth and eighteenth centuries, there was no recognition of a

clear demarcation between childhood and adolescence or between adolescence and adulthood. Life was short, and parents
showed little concern for the age of their children (Haeberle,
1977). The age of consent was low by today's standards; marriage
to children was not uncommon, and many girls were married by
age thirteen. Sleeping in the same bedroom or even the same bed
with parents was common up to the late 1600s, as was having
intercourse in the presence of children (Schultz, 1980). For centuries, the church, as the prevailing authoritarian body, showed
relatively little concern about the possibility of sexual activity
with or among children. In fact, since biblical times, the denial of
childhood sexuality was supported by the concept of "childhood
innocence," which was based on the belief that children were
asexual and thus had no sexual feelings or sexual capabilities
(Mrazek and Kempe, 1981).

The prevalence of incestuous activity, while impossible to document, can be assumed to have been high, based on the prevalence
of conditions now known to promote incest: social isolation such
as a rural society provides (Mrazek and Kempe, 1981; Summit
and Kryso, 1978); relative invisibility and unaccountability for
child-rearing practices to social authority; patriarchal family
structure and arbitrary paternal authority over children; con-
ceptualization of children as "property" without individual rights
of their own; absence of legal or social recourses for victims and
spouses to "report" such matters; and a relative lack of effective
social, religious, or legal reinforcements of the incest taboo.

In the sixteenth century, secular and ecclesiastical legal bodies
began to pass laws against selected aspects of child sexual abuse,
indicating that the problem had become extensive and visible
enough to initiate social concern. The limited nature and sequence of these laws tells us something about the previous views
and attitudes toward children and their sexual activity. As in mod-
ern times, what was obvious and violent provoked the first re-
actions, and incest was the last form of unsanctioned sexual practice to be addressed. Under the pressure of moralists, England
passed its first child protection laws: in 1548, sodomy with boys
was made illegal, and in 1576 forcible rape of girls under the age of
ten was made an offense punishable by death (Radzinowicz,

1948). The inferences here, of course, are that girls under ten could give legal consent to sexual relations with adults and that forcible rape of females over age ten was tolerable. In fact, English court records show, even up to 1880, that a charge of sexual assault could not be made if a girl gave voluntary consent to sexual intercourse, no matter what her age (Foster and Freed, 1964).

While incest was punishable under ecclesiastical courts, it did not become a criminal offense in England until 1908 (Manchester, 1979). Incest is today thought to be a transmittable phenomenon that promotes recurrence through subsequent generations (Brant and Tisza, 1977; Lustig et al., 1966). It is conceivable that indulgent attitudes toward sexual relations between children and adults went uncensured during the Middle Ages and were passed from generation to generation into the 1800s as part of the less visible "psychological inheritance," despite the proclamations of church and state. Under the Napoleonic Code during the late 1700s, France, followed by other European countries (except England), decriminalized some sexual behaviors and eased penalties for sex crimes against children. The result was a wave of increased tolerance and interest in the sexual exploitation of children. History documents that toward the end of the eighteenth century, pornography emphasizing adult-child sex and focusing on seduction and rape of children became increasingly popular. These events forced governments into defining adulthood through the establishment of an age of consent, which was followed by an ever-increasing need to raise the age of consent throughout the nineteenth century.

During this same period, the moralist movement in Western society grew more assertive in exerting influence upon child welfare. Pascal advised parents to control sexual molestation by supervising their children constantly, never leaving them alone with servants, avoiding nudity near adults, and enforcing modesty in the home (de Mause, 1974). A number of sexual superstitions eventually developed during this period, along with several laws regarding poorly defined sexual offenses against children. Children were seen as undisciplined animals who not only needed protection from their own sexual instincts but who also were "sexually dangerous" and tempting to adults. Victimized children were con-

sidered to be as responsible and as guilty as adult perpetrators of
sex crimes, and both were punished (Bullough, 1976). As the sup-
pression of childhood sexuality continued, concerted efforts were
made to prevent children from experiencing sexual arousal. The
dangers of masturbation became a major focus with explicit direc-
tives for parents to induce guilt in children for such behavior
(de Mause, 1974). Even children's literature came under censor-
ship (Aries, 1962). The goals of desexualizing children were supported by clergy, educators, and legal scholars, who became the
promoters of the new social conscience regarding adult-child sexual activities.

From a dynamic point of view, this zealous desexualizing process could very well have reflected an attempt to deal with prevalent temptations on the part of adults to commit sexual abuse of
children in the eighteenth and nineteenth centuries through denial, projection, and reaction formation. It suggests that just such
a perception may have existed in those small segments of society
that were in a position to promote moral codes and laws and to
impose penalties for sexual abuse of children.

In contrast to France, the United States and England maintained their strict orientation toward sexual misuse of children
with the gradual increasing of the age of consent throughout the
1800s. In 1861, the age of consent in England was raised to
twelve, and then in 1875 to thirteen, probably in response to growing concerns over the increase in sexual activity between adults
and pubescent children (West, 1974). By 1885, there had been
such a dramatic increase in prostitution among minors as a result
of spreading poverty and rural unemployment that the age of consent was raised to sixteen in a deliberate effort to control it
(Butler, 1954). From what has been learned in recent years about
sexual abuse, incest, and prostitution, it seems quite probable, in
retrospect, that the prevalence of incest (about which very little is
recorded in this period of history) was also extremely high in the
1800s. Survey studies have shown that a large percentage of child
prostitutes are derived from incestuous backgrounds (Bagley,
1984; James, 1977).

In the late nineteenth century, Freud observed that many of his
patients reported childhood memories of incidents of sexual se-

duction, often incestuous in nature. In 1896 Freud wrote: "Our children are far oftener exposed to sexual aggressions than we should suppose. . . . We might expect that increased attention to this subject would confirm the great frequency of sexual experiences and sexual activity in childhood" (Jones, 1959, p. 203). Freud shocked the medical community with this "seduction theory" that hysterical neurosis was caused by forgotten experiences of sexual abuse in childhood.

The implication that incestuous sexual misuse of children was prevalent among respectable families and contributed to a significant incidence of mental illness was felt to be intolerable and scandalous by the professional community of Freud's time. Freud was subjected to such overbearing pressures of professional ostracism and scorn that he repudiated the seduction theory within a year. In 1897 Freud put forth his new thesis that reports of sexual abuse made by his patients were not to be considered as factual but rather as derivatives of childhood fantasies representing repressed wishes and fears.

Subsequently, psychoanalysis focused more on the unconscious incestuous wishes and the role they played in the theories of infantile sexuality and the Oedipus complex rather than on overt incestuous acts (Lustig et al., 1966). However, this emphasis on the unconscious during the psychoanalytic period of psychiatry influenced many professionals to interpret as "fantasies" almost all patient symptoms and communications suggesting incest. Even among Freud's followers, case material pertaining to actual assaults on children was systematically censored. As Herman (1984) concluded, "Any further consideration of the possible validity of the seduction theory became a heresy within psychoanalysis" (p. 169). For years this prejudice of dynamic thinking pertaining to child sexual abuse supported a significant degree of professional incredulity and contributed to a "blind spot" in psychiatric history-taking and diagnostic assessments, a condition that has lasted throughout most of the twentieth century.

Views of the Twentieth Century

For more than two-thirds of this century, sexual child abuse has been perceived to be a minor social problem. Incest was thought to be rare and to exist primarily in isolated subcultures disassociated from the mainstream of society. This impression was supported (Weinberg, 1955) because the actual reported incidence of incest was quite low (about one case per million population). Sexual child abuse did not receive priority status in psychiatric research until the mid-1970s.

Epidemiological investigation continues to be limited by the covert nature of sexual abuse and the reluctance of individual victims, witnesses, and professionals to report incidents. Many of the current estimates are speculations based on limited and skewed data from statistics of court records, public service records, hospital and prison records, isolated clinical studies, and psychological questionnaires. Each approach has intrinsic value but also has inherent bias, which limits the reliability of extrapolation.

Data obtained from police and court records are perpetrator-oriented and reflect the inconsistent and oversimplified categorizations of sexual offenses affected by an orientation toward conviction. A categorical charge of "indecent liberties" may include a vague range of offenses from "obscene language" to "physical manipulation." Police records also contain a high percentage of cases of indecent exposure. The reluctance of family members to press charges and give testimony may influence police authorities to relegate cases of incest to charges of "indecent liberties" or "rape" in order to insure a conviction. Verifying physical examinations, specimen studies, and psychosocial histories are often absent.

Statistics from psychiatric hospitals are affected by the selectivity of victims who have a predilection to mental illness for a variety of reasons other than abuse. Furthermore, Peters (1976) found that most child abusers have no evidence of overt psychopathologic manifestations, and Summit and Kryso (1978) concluded that abusers are seldom psychotic. Studies of child abuse offenders among prisoners have the similar limitation of a nonrandom population, selected here by the process of arrest and conviction. Furthermore, many incarcerated offenders misrepresent their behavior, motivated by prospects of parole and by fear of reprisals from guards and prisonmates.

Emergency room and general hospital statistics predominantly include children who have incurred some degree of physical injury as an accompaniment to the sexual abuse, whereas it is generally acknowledged that most sexual abuse does not involve physical injury (Jason, Williams, Burton, and Rochat, 1982; Hicks, 1980; Finkelhor, 1979). In addition, their statistics include a greater proportion of extrafamilial sexual abuse as compared to incest, because more victims of extrafamilial sexual abuse are immediately brought to a physician or an emergency room. The more chronic cases of incest are rarely referred to a medical center (Brant and Tisza, 1977). It has also been found that hospital personnel and physicians have been inclined in the past, for many complex reasons, to underreport less conspicuous cases of sexual abuse. Children have been only infrequently tested for sexually transmitted diseases, resulting in many missed cases of sexual abuse (Kramer and Jason, 1982; White, Loda, and Ingram, 1983).

Clinical case studies by individual therapists have obvious statistical limitations; they frequently lack controls and standardized evaluations and have the predilection for "creative" bias.

Research utilizing random surveys of special groups is confounded by a self-selective process dependent upon the nature of willing volunteers, especially those having less need to repress and deny their past. Psychological questionnaires, usually of college students, are biased toward a more intellectually oriented and predominantly middle and upper middle class strata and may not be representative of the population at large.

Public service records tend to derive predominantly from the lower socioeconomic class (Mrazek and Kempe, 1981), where environmental factors may too easily be misinterpreted as fundamental to the findings. Greenberg (1979) concluded that statistical impressions of sexual abuse often reflect the nature of the population that is served by the particular public agency involved. Cultural mores may effect a willingness to report offenses, and false or exaggerated accusations by feuding family members, seeking custody or revenge, may distort and cloud the facts.

Hasty and superficial interviews upon which the data are based
often fail to fully clarify the nature of the act or the circumstances
involved, and they contain limited psychological and family histories of the victim and the perpetrator. Usually no follow-up
information exists upon which to make judgments of social and
psychological sequelae.

Current Understandings

Reports of sexual child abuse in Alabama have more than tri-
pled since 1975, when laws mandating the reporting first came
into existence. The dramatic increase in reports of sexual abuse
seems to reflect not only legal requirements but also an increase in
the willingness on the part of victims and their families to report
such occurrences. The impact of the attention given sexual child
abuse in the popular media and the increased openness and com-
fort on the part of parents and children to discuss sexual matters
certainly could contribute to the increased statistics as well. Even
sexually abused children are better able to conceptualize their experiences, have less need to maintain their secret, and are able to
communicate them more candidly (and, we hope, earlier).

A question troubling epidemiologists is whether an increase in
the actual incidence of sexual child abuse may have occurred during the past fifty years. A number of factors point to this possibility. Russell (1983) found in her survey that about twice as
many women in their twenties and thirties reported intrafamilial
childhood experiences of sexual abuse than did fifty- and sixty-
year-old women. No comparable increase of extrafamilial abuse
was reported in the same time period. This fact suggests that the
incidence of incestuous sexual abuse increased between the 1920s
and the 1950s. A number of conditions that have been found to
correlate with sexual child abuse have also increased during this
period. The increase in the numbers of divorces, single-parent
families, and remarriages has been dramatic in the past fifty
years. Daughters of divorced mothers have a greater incidence of
sexual abuse than girls of intact families (Finkelhor, 1979); divorced mothers who are dating actively may put their daughters in
jeopardy by bringing more sexually opportunistic men into the

home. Research consistently shows that children living with a stepfather or mother's boyfriend have more than double the risk of sexual abuse than those living with a natural father (Finkelhor, 1979). Russell (1984) found that, among women who had a stepfather, one out of six was sexually abused by him, whereas only one out of forty women living with a biological father was abused. Girls with stepfathers are also at risk of exposure to more predatory males and are five times more likely to be victimized by a friend of their parents.

Finkelhor (1984) stated that one of the major effects of the sexual revolution has been the erosion of traditional, externalized controls over sexual behavior. The late 1970s saw a sudden increase in pornography portraying children as sex objects (Baker, 1978; Burgess, 1982, 1984; Dillingham and Melmed, 1982; Tyler, 1982). It is feared that child prostitution has significantly escalated in recent years as well; estimates of the number of children currently involved in prostitution and pornography range from 300,000 to 600,000. Prostitution and pornography both tend to derive a significant percentage of participants from incestuous families, and both contribute to the promotion of extrafamilial sexual abuse. James (1977) reported that 22 percent of a group of prostitutes admitted to incestuous sexual experiences.

An area of research speculation is the effect of the women's liberation movement upon vulnerable males in terms of their intimidation and their resulting inclination to turn to more passive and more easily dominated children, a characteristic feature in the histories of regressive pedophilia (Peters and Sadoff, 1970).

From the foregoing discussion, it would appear that the occurrence of sexual abuse would be influenced less than physical abuse by the hypothesized geographical or cultural conditions. In order to test this theory, the following epidemiological investigation of sexual child abuse in Alabama (which was affected by many of the limitations mentioned above) analyzed the reporting and abuse characteristics in the three community types described in chapter 2.

PART TWO
Child Abuse in Alabama:
An Epidemiological Investigation

4
The Context and Methodology
of the Study

In 1963, the United States Children's Bureau drafted a model child abuse reporting law, and within only a few years every state had adopted a mandatory reporting statute. Alabama's version, Act No. 563, passed in 1965, mandated reporting by "all hospitals, clinics, sanitariums, doctors, physicians, surgeons, nurses, school teachers, pharmacists, social workers, or any other person called upon to render aid or medical assistance." Within a decade, the U.S. Senate Subcommittee on Children and Youth had held a series of hearings on child abuse, and in 1974 Congress passed Public Law 93–247, also known as the Mondale Act or as the National Child Abuse Prevention and Treatment Act. In response to this federal initiative, in 1975 the Alabama legislature amended and reenacted Act No. 563 through the passage of the Child Abuse and Neglect Reporting Law (Act No. 1124).

Alabama's Child Abuse and Neglect Reporting Law

The importance of the 1975 reporting law cannot be overstated. Intervention in child abuse can be activated only by reports of suspected abuse and neglect, and, likewise, prevention strategies can only be effective if they address known risk factors. Act No. 1124 identifies exactly who is required to make reports and the penalty for their failure to do so. The duties of the Department of Pensions and Security (DPS) upon receipt of a report are clearly defined. Sections of the law pertinent to this research are summarized here.

Section 1 defined abuse as "harm or threatened harm to a

child's health or welfare [which can occur through] non-accidental physical or mental injury; sexual abuse, or attempted sexual abuse." The definition of a child in this 1975 law included any person under eighteen years of age.

Section 3 expanded the specific categories of persons required to make reports; in addition to those mentioned in the 1965 law were medical examiners, coroners, dentists, osteopaths, optometrists, chiropractors, podiatrists, peace officers, law enforcement officials, and mental health professionals.

Section 4, "permissive reporting," stated that all other persons not listed in Section 3 may make abuse and neglect reports, though they are not required to do so.

Section 7, a major addition to the law, outlined the duties of the Department of Pensions and Security following receipt of a report of child abuse or neglect. The section stated:

> The state or county department of pensions and security shall make a thorough investigation promptly upon either the oral or written report . . . [which] shall include:
> (1) The nature, extent and cause of the child abuse or neglect;
> (2) The identity of the person responsible therefor[e];
> (3) The names and conditions of other children in the home;
> (4) An evaluation of the parents or person responsible for the care of the child;
> (5) The home environment and the relationship of the child or children to the parents or other persons responsible for their care; and
> (6) All other data deemed pertinent.

Section 8 of the law established a central registry within the Department of Pensions and Security for the purpose of storing all reports of child abuse and neglect. Section 8 stated:

> (a) The state department of pensions and security shall establish a statewide central registry for reports of child abuse and neglect made pursuant to this [Act]. The central registry shall contain, but shall not be limited to:
> (1) All information in the written report;
> (2) Record of the final disposition of the report, including services offered and services accepted;

    (3) The names and identifying data, dates and circumstances of
any persons requesting or receiving information from the
registry;

    (4) The plan for rehabilitative treatment; and

    (5) Any other information which might be helpful in furthering
the purposes of [the Act].

In addition to establishing the registry, section 8 defined the rules
of confidentiality and use of the registry and reports as follows:

    (b) The state department of pensions and security shall establish
and enforce reasonable rules and regulations governing the
custody, use and preservation of the reports and records of child
abuse and neglect. The use of such reports and records shall be
limited to the purposes for which they are furnished and by the
provisions of law under which they may be furnished. The reports
and records of child abuse and neglect shall be confidential, and
shall not be used or disclosed for any purposes other than: . . .

        (5) For use by any person engaged in bona fide research who is
authorized to have access to such information by the commissioner of the state department of pensions and security.

In 1977, the Alabama Child Abuse Act (Alabama Code
26–15–1) made the commission of child abuse a criminal offense
punishable by "imprisonment in the penitentiary for not less than
one year nor more than ten years," and in 1981, Act No. 81–789
expanded the definition of abuse to include sexual exploitation or
attempted sexual exploitation.

In 1975, the year in which the Child Abuse and Neglect Reporting Law was passed, the Department of Pensions and Security
received 887 reports of neglect and abuse; in 1984 the number of
reports exceeded 28,000. Each report filed in the registry had followed a similar sequence of steps as it passed through the system.
Familiarity with the route is important to an understanding of the
analyses that follow.

Briefly, when a report of child abuse is made to a county DPS
office, an intake worker completes Form PSD-BFC 959 (see appendix A), detailing information about the child or children who
were allegedly victimized, the parents and siblings, the alleged

perpetrator, the relationship of the person making the report (if he or she chooses to be identified), and a brief description of the incident prompting the report. This form (Form 959) distinguishes only between neglect and abuse; the differentiation between sexual and physical abuse is found only in the narrative description of the incident that is completed after an investigation is made. One copy of Form 959 is mailed to the central registry; at the same time, another copy is transferred to a county caseworker for investigation of the allegation. This investigation may involve repeated trips to the household and interviews with the family members or others living with them.

After completing the investigation, the caseworker files a narrative report that includes a determination of the case, that is, whether the case is declared confirmed, unfounded, or undetermined. A case is declared founded when the caseworker is able to collect sufficient evidence that abuse or neglect has occurred; it is declared undetermined when the caseworker has some doubts remaining but sufficient evidence is not available for confirmation; and a case is declared unfounded when the caseworker finds that the allegation is false or finds no evidence to substantiate the report. A copy of the narrative investigation report is then mailed to the central registry, where it is affixed to the original Form 959 sent when the report was first received. After the narrative is received by the department, a clerk completes two items heretofore left blank on the 959 form: (1) whether the case was declared founded, unfounded, or undetermined, and (2) whether the child was summarily removed. These reports are filed in the central registry according to the county and the year in which the incident occurred. In fiscal year 1982 (October 1, 1981, through September 30, 1982), the year chosen for our study, 20,213 reports were filed in the DPS Central Registry.

The Study Methodology

The 1975 reporting statute provided a mechanism for the documentation and storage of information about child abuse and its characteristics. Data for this study were drawn from fiscal year

1982 reports of child abuse and neglect (CAN) filed in the Department of Pensions and Security Central Registry.

RESEARCH QUESTIONS AND STUDY VARIABLES

As described previously, this research was undertaken to test the hypothesis that community size contributes to a unique picture of surveillance, reporting, and caseworker determination of abuse. Specifically, this research was designed (1) to determine the incidence of child abuse and neglect in the state of Alabama and to identify the characteristics of confirmed child abuse, and (2) to compare the statewide results with results specific to three distinct geopolitical units—rural areas, towns and small cities, and urban places. The questions guiding this research were therefore descriptive in nature. Specifically, we wanted to find out who makes the reports of abuse, who is abused, who commits that abuse, and what happens to the child once a report is received. The variables that address these research questions can be divided into six fairly distinct categories as follows. (Data were insufficient for analysis of those variables that are marked by an asterisk.)

1. Reporter variables
   a. who made the report, i.e., the reporter's relationship to the child
   b. to whom the report was made (DPS, police, or sheriff)
2. Victim variables
   a. sex
   b. race
   c. age
   d. birth order
   e. number of siblings, their age and sex
   f. personal characteristics, i.e., intelligence, academic record, behavior record, etc.*
   g. injuries resulting from the abuse
3. Household characteristics and family variables
   a. identified head of family
   b. number of children in the household

     c. number of adults in the household
     d. marital status of the parents
     e. age of the parents*
     f. educational level of the parents*
     g. socioeconomic level of the household*
     h. employment of adult household members*
     i. social and medical history of the parents (e.g., criminal record, mental illness, etc.)*
     j. alcohol and drug use of household members*
     k. previous neglect or abuse reports*
4. Perpetrator variables
     a. sex
     b. age
     c. race
     d. relationship to child
     e. employment status*
     f. social and medical history (as above)*
     g. alcohol and drug use*
     h. previous neglect and abuse reports*
5. Incident variables
     a. kind of abuse (physical, sexual, emotional)
     b. where the abuse occurred (victim's home, relative's home, etc.)
     c. disposition of the abuse incident
6. Community and county characteristic variables
     a. size of community/county
     b. racial composition of community/county
     c. unemployment rates, crime rates, etc. of county
     d. percentage living below poverty level in community/county

SAMPLE SELECTION

Sampling techniques are employed in research for two principal reasons: (1) to reduce the total research population to a manageable number (due to cost and time), and (2) to assure a representative selection from the total. In this study, the choice of sampling strategy was complicated due to the lack of any knowledge about the contents of the central registry. It was not known, for example, what proportions of reports represented neglect or abuse or how many reports were founded, unfounded, or undetermined.

The DPS system and mandatory reporting laws (which make the study of reported abuse possible) are based upon the county unit: reports are made to county offices, investigations are conducted by county caseworkers, and cases are filed by the county unit. The county, rather than the case, was chosen as the primary sampling unit. This decision carried with it the major advantage that large amounts of data concerning relevant social and environmental characteristics are readily available on county units.

In order to select an adequately representative sample from the sixty-seven Alabama counties, the social and environmental characteristics suggested in the literature as contributing to the occurrence of child abuse (e.g., poverty, broken families, single parents, urban living, unemployment, violence, and amount of education) were identified for each county. Statistics on these variables were obtained for each county through the United States Census Bureau and numerous state agency publications.

These multiple characteristics were factor analyzed so as to reduce them to shared underlying dimensions. Four factors were obtained, derived by varimax rotation. Two strong factors, accounting for 59 and 28 percent of the variance, respectively, were retained and are the factor loadings presented in Table 4–1. Factor 1 describes the urbanicity of the county and Factor 2 describes county wealth. Surprisingly, the unemployment rate loaded alone on Factor 4; it had a loading of only $-.14931$ on Factor 1 and $+.00353$ on Factor 2. The percentage of persons owning their own homes originally loaded negatively on Factor 1 and positively on Factor 2, but, due to the high level of home ownership among the rural poor and the low level among city dwellers, it was dropped from the final factor analysis.

Factor scores were assigned to each of the sixty-seven Alabama counties; the counties were then sorted by factor scores. This procedure allowed the counties to be economically described in relation to both factors (which could be considered composite descriptions of the state) as well as in relation to one another. The

Table 4–1

Factor Loadings

County Characteristics	Factor 1	Factor 2
Urban population (%)	.79233	.14100
Persons per square mile	.76835	.22161
Median income	.51216	.76691
Population below poverty level (%)	−.25579	−.92827
Female–headed households (%)	.25980	−.90557
Median years of schooling	.66114	.34075
Divorce rate	.38695	.44326
Crimes against persons rate	.65475	.34772
Property crime rate	.93969	.00025

factors were each divided into quintiles and combined by identifying groups based upon the counties' relative positions along the two factors. For example, counties in the highest quintile on Factor 1 and the highest quintile on Factor 2 formed one group, counties in the highest quintile on Factor 1 and in the lowest quintile on Factor 2 formed another group, and so forth. Counties falling into the same group were, therefore, sociologically and environmentally similar. Finally, one county was randomly selected from each of the twenty-five resulting groups in order to form the final sample, which is shown in Figure 4–1. The resulting study sample closely represents the state of Alabama on important demographic variables, as shown in Table 4–2. All reports of abuse and neglect from the twenty-five sample counties were subsequently reviewed.

DATA COLLECTION

Due to gross underfunding and understaffing, the DPS Central

Table 4-2

Comparison of Study Sample and Alabama Demographic Characteristics

Demographic Characteristics	Study Sample (25 Counties)	State of Alabama (67 Counties)
Black population (%)	26.31	25.50
Female-headed households (%)	14.67	14.85
Living with two parents (%)	73.40	72.98
Median years of schooling	11.38	11.45
Median family income (in dollars)	14.64	14.58
Population living below poverty (%)	18.35	18.22
Persons per square mile (%)	73.10	72.50
Property crime rate*	2,319.00	2,466.00
Unemployment rate**	11.02	11.60
Violent crime rate*	266.00	278.00

*   offenses known to police per 100,000 population
** per 100 civilian work force

Registry is, in fact, no more than a small filing room in which CAN reports are stored alphabetically by county in manilla folders. Approximately two-thirds of the 1982 reports included a 959 form attached to its corresponding caseworker narrative. The remaining 959 forms and narratives were randomly (i.e., separately) filed. For example, 1,591 reports had been received from Jefferson County, each consisting of a 959 and a narrative; these had been filed in at least twenty manilla folders. In other words, there were 3,182 separate documents, each of which would ideally be filed with its match but which were often, in fact, located sepa-

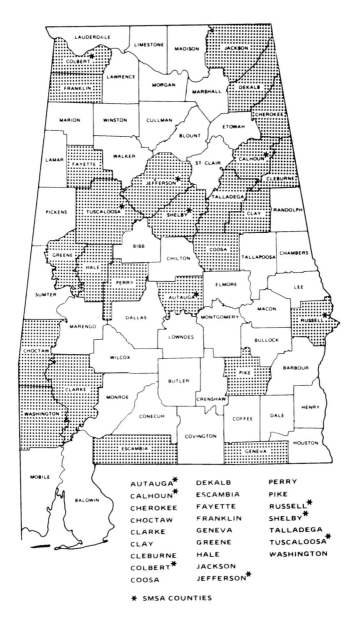

LAUDERDALE · LIMESTONE · MADISON · JACKSON
COLBERT · LAWRENCE · MORGAN · MARSHALL · DEKALB
FRANKLIN · CHEROKEE
MARION · WINSTON · CULLMAN · ETOWAH
BLOUNT
LAMAR · WALKER · ST CLAIR · CALHOUN
FAYETTE · JEFFERSON · CLEBURNE
TALLADEGA
PICKENS · TUSCALOOSA · SHELBY · CLAY · RANDOLPH
BIBB · COOSA
GREENE · CHILTON · TALLAPOOSA · CHAMBERS
HALE · ELMORE · LEE
PERRY · AUTAUGA
SUMTER · DALLAS · MACON
MARENGO · MONTGOMERY · RUSSELL
LOWNDES · BULLOCK
CHOCTAW · WILCOX · BARBOUR
CLARKE · BUTLER · PIKE
MONROE · CRENSHAW · HENRY
WASHINGTON · CONECUH · COFFEE · DALE
COVINGTON
ESCAMBIA · GENEVA · HOUSTON
MOBILE
BALDWIN

AUTAUGA*	DEKALB	PERRY
CALHOUN*	ESCAMBIA	PIKE
CHEROKEE	FAYETTE	RUSSELL*
CHOCTAW	FRANKLIN	SHELBY*
CLARKE	GENEVA	TALLADEGA
CLAY	GREENE	TUSCALOOSA*
CLEBURNE	HALE	WASHINGTON
COLBERT*	JACKSON	
COOSA	JEFFERSON*	

* SMSA COUNTIES

Figure 4–1   The Study Sample

rately in different folders. When a narrative report could not be located by the research team, DPS record room personnel assisted in a search for the report; when it could not be located by either group, the case was recorded as incomplete. The final number of incomplete reports was small, but to arrive at this number required an amount of time that would easily argue against replication.

Data were collected by the researchers with the assistance of two additional office staff members. All persons involved were trained in the use of the data collection forms, and their work was closely observed during the first day of data collection and was spot-checked thereafter. Data collection took a total of 250 workhours; in other words, one person working alone would have taken more than five weeks to collect the data. The reliability of the data collection procedure and the accuracy of the multiple data collectors were assessed by reviewing a random selection of 100 reports for accuracy and comprehensiveness. Only one data collector was found to have any inaccuracies; all forms completed by that person were subsequently reviewed and corrected when necessary.

DATA COLLECTION FORMS

Two data collection forms were designed for this study. The first form was prepared for a tally of founded, unfounded, and undetermined neglect cases in each sampled county. A similar form was used to tally the unfounded and undetermined sexual and physical abuse cases.

The Confirmed Abuse Form (see appendix B), designed for this study of confirmed sexual and physical abuse, mirrored DPS Form 959 (the abuse and neglect report intake form) but included additional items for collecting information from the caseworker's narrative description of the incident of abuse. These items were chosen for inclusion based on a variety of sources: (1) a thorough search of the literature to determine both empirically derived and suggested correlates of abuse, (2) suggestions from DPS administrative personnel, social workers, and physicians who have had professional experience with abuse cases, and (3) the DPS investigatory requirements as outlined by the reporting statute. As indicated above, much of the information on these variables was not sufficient for analysis. In all, the Confirmed Abuse Form included 162 variables.

CODING

All cases of neglect and all unfounded and undetermined cases of abuse were counted for the twenty-five sampled counties. The Confirmed Abuse Form was coded for computer analysis. In addition, the following information was gathered concerning the town in which the incident of abuse occurred: the population size, the percentage of black population, the percentage living below the poverty level (according to the 1980 census), and the percentage of increase or decrease in population over the last decade.

ANALYSIS

Several computer files were maintained for analysis. All cases (black/white, male/female, sexual/physical abuse) were added to the county file for the purpose of calculating abuse rates. Two additional files were constructed: one used the report (regardless of the number of children it included) as the unit of analysis, while the second used each victim of abuse as a unit of analysis. In other words, the first file was used for the analysis of the incident, the perpetrator, or the reporter of abuse, whereas the second file was used for all analyses of the victims (their age, sex, race, etc.). Using two such files prevented distortions and misrepresentations from occurring as would happen, for example, if a father who abused eight children were tallied as eight perpetrators. The same type of distortion was avoided in counting the frequency of sources of reports, types of households, marital status of the parents, and so forth.

This study generated descriptive frequency data. As previously mentioned, most 959 forms were missing information on one or more items. Therefore, when the results of cross-tabulations are presented, the numbers may vary due to these missing data. This problem is exacerbated by each additional variable tabulated. The data were analyzed by frequency tabulation and, where indicated, by Chi-square. Relationships between county characteristics and abuse rates were analyzed by correlation techniques.

5
Social and Cultural
Modifiers of Reporter
and Caseworker Determinations

Before a case of abuse can be entered into a calculation of abuse rates, it must pass through two filters, the reporter and the investigator/caseworker. The final rates and the calculation of risk factors depend less upon the accuracy of the report than upon the similarity in definition used by the reporter and the caseworker. Research results based on reported cases may confound the hypothesized factors associated with abuse with those associated with reporting and caseworker determination, as discussed in chapter 2. This chapter will investigate the effect of the reporter and caseworker filters on the calculation of epidemiological estimates in Alabama. In addition, the relationship between these two filters and the various hypothesized social and cultural correlates of abuse will be discussed.

Both reports and investigations of abuse are made within the context and system of individual counties. The social setting of counties is, therefore, likely to influence which cases finally enter into the calculation of abuse rates. Comparing the intermediate figures as cases pass through each of these two filters (the reporter and the caseworker) to become rates of abuse provides a means of determining the relationship of county characteristics to each stage.[1]

The reporter, the first screen or "filter" through which abuse is made known, is one key to understanding the social-contextual factors that contribute to the process of defining a "case." The reporter, however, is only the first screen or filter. Once the report is made to the county DPS office, a caseworker, who is a second powerful filter, is assigned to investigate the allegation of abuse. In making an assessment (e.g., founded, unfounded, or undetermined), caseworkers draw upon their training and experience, upon the legal (but not operationalized) definition of abuse, upon their own histories and cultural values, and upon their length of time in the field; in other words, caseworkers are propelled toward a determination by differing sets of definitions. Abuse at its most extreme, such as in the case of fractures or death, probably presents few problems of definition, but many more cases are less clear.

The literature hardly addresses this issue. In reference to the medical diagnosis of abuse, Newberger and Daniel (1976) argued that the heavily value-laden confirmation of abuse is made more easily "when the clinical setting is public and there is great social distance (social class or ethnic discrepancy) between clinician and family" (p. 19). The same must be true for the caseworker. Jason, Andereck, Marks, and Tyler (1982) compared confirmed (N = 4,221) and ruled-out (N = 1,891) reports for July 1975 through December 1979 from the statewide computerized Georgia Child Abuse Registry in order to separate risk factors from reporting bias. Their analysis was based upon the important assumption that the investigator's classification of a case into confirmed or ruled-out categories is "a more accurate assessment of whether abuse occurred than is the suspicion of someone reporting the case to the system" (p. 1353). Increased risk was associated with a characteristic only when that characteristic was more prevalent in the confirmed than in the ruled-out category (such as large families, white two-parent households, and black female-headed households). Unfortunately, however, the analysis does not investigate the effects of "assessment biases," that is, caseworker definitions of abuse.

Garbarino and Crouter (1978) tested the hypothesis that construct validity of reporting units would "presume" an inverse relationship (negative correlation) between socioeconomic resources and the rate of child maltreatment. Using three distinct sets of data, the authors compared origins of reports over time, urban areas versus rural areas, and homicide rates versus child abuse rates. They concluded that "the socioeconomic criterion may provide a necessary condition for establishing the validity of report data" (p. 599). Their study, however, used socioeconomic status as a criterion of reporter validity without differentiating between reports declared founded and those declared unfounded; in other words, they did not address the issue of caseworker validity.

Because hospital personnel are professionally trained to identify the cause of disease or injury, they effectively fill the dual role of reporter and investigator. Nonetheless, in a study of hospital recognition and reporting of abuse based upon data drawn from the National Study of the Incidence and Severity of Child Abuse and Neglect (Department of Health and Human Services, 1981), Hampton and Newberger (1985) concluded that significant underreporting occurred (less than half the cases), as did notable biases in reporting by class and race.

As shown in Table 5–1, the rate of reporting and the rate of abuse in Alabama are positively and significantly correlated. The percentage of confirmed reports, however, is negatively correlated with the report rate and virtually uncorrelated with the abuse rate. In other words, counties with higher report rates have lower percentages of confirmation and vice versa. The number of cases per capita after confirmation is not correlated with the proportion of all reports that are confirmed.

Analyzing these rates individually, reported physical abuse (prior to caseworker determination) is significantly and negatively

Table 5–1

Correlations of Physical Abuse Report Rates, Percentages of Reports Confirmed, and Final Abuse Rates

	Report Rate	% of Reports Confirmed	Final Abuse Rate
Report rate	(1.00)	___	___
% of reports confirmed	$-.51^{*}$	(1.00)	___
Final abuse rate	$.67^{**}$	.14	(1.00)

* $p < .05$
** $p < .001$

correlated with such county characteristics as percentage of black
population, percentage of population living below the poverty

Table 5–2

Correlations of Physical Abuse Report Rates, Percentages of Reports
Confirmed, and Confirmed Abuse Rates with Selected County
Characteristics

County Characteristics	Report Rate	% Reports Confirmed	Confirmed Abuse Rate
Black population (%)	−.38***	.61*	.05
Crime	−.06	−.08	−.00
Divorce rate	.25	−.40***	.12
Factor score 1 (urbanness)	−.14	−.06	−.03
Factor score 2 (wealth)	.06	−.35***	−.11
Female–headed households (%)	−.36***	.55**	.33
Home ownership (%)	−.07	−.09	−.27
Living with two parents (%)	.33***	−.51**	−.25
Median years of schooling	−.02	−.21	−.06
Persons per square mile	−.11	−.14	−.13
Poverty level (% below)	−.40***	.66*	−.08
Unemployment rate	−.39***	.21	.09
Urban population (% of inhabitants living in places of 2500 or more)	.15	−.27	.14

* p < .001
** p < .01
*** p < .05

level, percentage of female-headed households, and the unemployment rate, as shown in the first column of Table 5–2. In other words, counties ranked high on these characteristics produce a proportionately lower number of reports. All other county characteristics are unrelated to abuse report rates.

When a report of suspected abuse is made to county welfare offices, a caseworker within the county system is assigned to investigate the report. Comparing the counties' different percentages of confirmation based on the total number of reports received provides an indication of caseworker variability between counties. The average of confirmed physical abuse reports in the twenty-five sample counties is 39 percent (SD = 19); the actual percentages ranged from 11 to 100. A higher percentage of confirmation may indicate a true characteristic of risk (the premise underlying the 1982 study by Jason, Andereck, Marks, and Tyler) or, alternatively, may indicate a caseworker definition of abuse more consonant with reporters' definitions in these contexts and thus a more porous filter. As shown in the center column in Table 5–2, the percentage of total cases confirmed is significantly and positively correlated with the percentages of blacks, poverty level, and female-headed households, while it is significantly and negatively correlated with two-parent households and with the county divorce rate. (Divorce rate is highest in counties in Alabama in which there is a low percentage of blacks.)

A factor analysis of the county (N = 67) characteristics produced four factors, explained in detail in the preceding chapter. Factors 1 and 2, which were derived by varimax rotation and accounted for 59 and 28 percent of the variance, respectively, conceptually identified the "urbanness" of the county (Factor 1) and the county wealth (Factor 2). While Factor 1 scores are not correlated with either reports or the percentage of confirmed reports, scores from Factor 2 are negatively correlated with the percentage of reported cases that were confirmed by caseworkers. When rates of physical abuse are calculated (number of confirmed cases divided by population at risk), all of these correlations disappear, indicating that no linear relationship exists between the actual numbers of confirmed cases per capita and the county characteristics; in other words, the final number of cases (the confirmed

cases) is not related to the percentage of black population, the
percentage living below the poverty level, and so forth. In sexual
abuse, neither the report rate nor the abuse rate is correlated with
the county characteristics; only the percentage of all reports confirmed is significantly and positively related to black, poor, and
female-headed households and negatively related to the percentage of two-parent households.

Implications

Epidemiological findings are utilized to identify groups at risk.
A surveillance-to-determination system free of systematic error
would predict an abuse rate to be positively correlated with the
report rate and with the proportion or percentage of cases confirmed. These correlations in this study do not follow the expected
pattern. If we were to calculate rates based upon reports, we
would conclude that only two-parent households are at risk;
blacks, the poor, the unemployed, and female-headed households
would appear to be characteristics contrary to abuse. On the
other hand, if we look only at the proportion of cases confirmed,
there is clear risk in predominantly black, poor, and female-
headed households. After reports have passed through this caseworker filter and only the remaining founded cases are used in the
calculation of rates, all of these relationships simply disappear
and we would conclude that there are no socioeconomic risk factors. This threefold and dramatic shift in relationships will un-
questionably have some influence on any predictions about risk
factors associated with "true" abuse.

Gil (1969) and Pelton (1978) have argued that sufficient epidemiological evidence that child abuse is concentrated among the
poor outweighs the effects of probable reporter bias. It is interesting that in the Alabama study, rates of reporting are, in fact,
lowest in the predominantly poor and black counties; the percentages of confirmed cases, however, are highest there. In other
words, no reporter bias exists against the poor in Alabama; in
fact, these data indicate a reporter bias for the poor. Potential reporters in counties with the greatest chronic poverty may feel the
most threatened by, and disillusioned with, the benevolence of the

"welfare system." Poverty may also affect a potential reporter by elevating the threshold at which the treatment of a child is judged as maltreatment. The reversal in correlation of reporting and of confirmation with poverty would support these conclusions. Applying the Garbarino and Crouter (1978) model developed to test reporter validity, these data would confirm the socioeconomic criterion only with respect to the percentage of cases confirmed, that is, caseworker validity but not reporter validity. Caseworkers who are by training and by occupation intellectually and financially separated from the culture of poverty more often define as founded abuse those reports originating in impoverished areas. It is plausible to hypothesize, after observing these sizable shifts in the direction and strength of correlations, that the caseworkers' determinations are biased against the poor.

Although the counties with few reports had high confirmation percentages, the total numbers of cases remained low. Conversely, counties with high numbers of reports had a smaller percentage confirmed, and the final yield was a similarly low number of confirmed cases. These relationships would also explain the moderately high correlation between the percentage confirmed and the rate of abuse. The possibility also exists that counties with investigations approaching unmanageable numbers might employ more stringent criteria for confirming physical abuse.

In spite of the obvious fact that all counties have potentially numerous and equivalent reporters within each category, unexplained variability remains in the sources of reports that are confirmed. In four counties, all of the confirmed reports of black physical abuse were reported to the system by relatives of the victim; in three counties, all of the confirmed cases were reported by institutions. Other categories of reporters were not represented within these counties; in the former, confirmable institutional reports were nonexistent, and in the latter, relatives and "concerned citizens" did not make confirmable reports. Potential reporters, even those who live in communities in which abuse may be prevalent, are less likely to make a report if the visibility or known availability of child welfare services is low. On the other hand, in communities in which the actual incidence of abuse is low, citizens may report more frequently if services are well known and are perceived as accessible. Members of the middle and upper classes generally view child welfare agencies as resources appropriate only for the poor, while those living in poverty consider these agencies to be "police" agencies that control their pursestrings and have the power to remove their children. Recognizing these conditions, can we assume (as indicated in the literature) that black children are actually at greater risk of abuse in the more highly complex areas, such as cities, or is there only a greater likelihood of the abuse being *reported* there? Are whites at greater risk of being abused or are they more likely to be *reported* in the smaller, less complex communities?

The person who makes a report that is later declared unfounded or undetermined, especially if he or she is a relative or neighbor of the victim, may have a definition of abuse more culturally valid than does the caseworker, who is usually an outsider. In other words, the caseworker has the authority to deny abuse even when the persons closest to the incident affirm it. Abuse reported by an institution, on the other hand, represents professionals in dialogue and the greater likelihood of similar definitions. These observations support the conclusion by Starbuck et al. (1984), following their study of child abuse in Hawaii, that a need exists for consideration of regional and cultural variations when investigating and screening for child abuse. Chapters 7 and 8 look at the specific and varied reporting patterns in Alabama's rural, midsized, and urban areas.

Notes

1. The following formulas were used in the calculations:

$$\text{Report rate} = \frac{\text{total \# reports}}{\text{population under 18}}$$

$$\% \text{ reports confirmed} = \frac{\text{confirmed reports}}{\text{total \# reports}} \times 100$$

$$\text{Abuse rate} = \frac{\text{\# confirmed}}{\text{population under 18}}$$

6
The Sources of Reports

Physical Abuse

As mentioned in chapter 4, reports activate child abuse investigations and are, therefore, critical to any understanding of child abuse incidence. Reports also provide clues to the level of responsibility that a community assumes toward the treatment of its children. As predicted, the sources of physical abuse reports in this study varied considerably with the size of the community, suggesting differential strengths and weaknesses within the respective surveillance systems. (Unfortunately, data here included only cases of abuse confirmed by the caseworker, thus precluding any comparative analysis of confirmed versus unfounded abuse characteristics.) This chapter will describe the sources of reports statewide, followed by a comparison of the reporting networks of Alabama's rural areas, towns and small cities, and urbanized areas.

Unlike states outside the South, the history of the state of Alabama has been largely defined by two major ethnic or racial groups, black and white. They share a cultural experience, but, at the same time, each group has developed important and distinct cultural differences. These broad cultural traditions, which include attitudes toward marriage and raising children, are modified by the social and economic realities of daily experience within one's smaller community. This investigation into the incidence of physical abuse supports the influence of these cultural and community differences.

49

THE SOURCES OF REPORTS STATEWIDE

Table 6–1 shows the percentages of all sources of reports of physical abuse by the race of the child. For black children, professional groups, such as social workers, hospitals, and especially schools (21 percent), accounted for almost half of all confirmed abuse reporters. White children, on the other hand, were gener-

Table 6–1

Statewide Percentages of Sources of Reports of Physical Abuse by Race* of Victim

Reporting Source	Black (N=223)		White (N=346)	
Relative	23.2		29.2	
Mother		6.7		11.6
Father		3.6		2.6
Grandparent		4.5		7.5
Uncle		.4		.9
Aunt		7.6		4.3
Sibling		.4		.6
Stepparent		—		1.7
Institution	42.5		31.5	
Police		2.2		4.9
Sheriff		1.8		.6
Clergy		.4		.6
Social worker		6.3		5.5
School		20.6		10.1
Physician		1.8		2.9
Hospital		9.4		6.9
Other	16.1		21.9	
Friends/neighbors		13.0		15.3
Other**		3.1		6.6
Anonymous	12.6		12.1	
Self	5.8			5.2

* X^2=8.75; df=4; p=.06
** includes landlords, shopkeepers, employers, babysitters, etc.

ally referred to the system by nonprofessionals. These reporters were somewhat more vigilant of, or more willing to report, abuse of white children: relatives as a group and friends and/or neighbors of the child accounted for 45 percent of the reports.

It appears, therefore, that greater surveillance of black than white children was made by professionals, the groups mandated by Alabama law to report abuse. It is known that black families utilize hospital emergency rooms more frequently than white families, which could, at least in part, account for the greater frequency of hospital reports. The larger proportion of black reports from educators, however, cannot be similarly explained. It is noteworthy that physicians not based in hospitals accounted for an insignificant proportion of reports of either race, in spite of the likelihood that they frequently treat victims of abuse.

Several interesting patterns emerge when comparing the source of the report and the victim and perpetrator of the abuse. For example, with the exception of mothers and aunts, all sources tended to report black boys more often than girls; black mothers reported abuse of their daughters in almost 75 percent of their reports. Markedly different, however, was the tendency of white mothers and fathers to report abuse of their sons (68 and 70 percent, respectively). Only police, schools, and anonymous persons reported white girls more frequently than they did white boys.

Thirty-one reports were received from the victims themselves. White girls reported their own victimization five times more often than did white boys, black girls twice as often as black boys. The thirteen black children reported their mothers in almost half the cases; they reported their fathers and stepfathers less frequently. The eighteen white children who made self-reports accused, in almost equal proportions, their fathers, mothers, stepfathers, and stepmothers of the abuse.

When a father of either race was the identified abuser, the child's mother reported him in only one-fifth of the cases. In spite of the fact that the most frequent family type for white abuse is the child's original biological family, mothers very rarely (20 percent) reported the father; friends and neighbors made almost as many reports of white fathers as did the child's mother. Among blacks, neither the mother nor the neighbors reported fathers very often, due in part to the absence of a father, as evidenced by the greater percentage (55 percent) of black households headed by women.

When white mothers were identified as the perpetrators, the report generally originated outside the family—in the schools (16 percent), hospitals (9 percent), others (11 percent), or unknown (10 percent). Abusive black mothers were also identified most frequently by outsiders, that is, by the school system (24 percent) and by neighbors (16 percent). Schools seemed more alert to abuse of black children than to that of white children, although it is impossible to separate surveillance and reporting.

COMPARISON OF COMMUNITY SIZE AND SOURCES OF REPORTS

The population of Alabama is largely rural; 49 percent of the state's residents live in rural areas (including towns of fewer than 10,000 inhabitants). Residents of rural areas, however, made only 42 percent (N = 238) of the reports of physical abuse of children. Rural people are more likely to know their neighbors and to share a sense of community with them, especially in areas where there is no large town or city nearby. Newcomers to these areas are rare, and most residents generally belong to one of a few extended families. Do these conditions of familiarity lead to higher rates of reporting because people know one another and are aware of problems, to lower rates of reporting because people are reluctant to report someone they know, or are rural people simply more accepting of abuse? Or does the sense of community they share mobilize an informal helping network?

More than half (56 percent) of Alabama's white population under eighteen years old live in these rural areas and were the subjects of 52 percent of the white physical abuse in the state. Among blacks under eighteen years old, 41 percent live in rural areas, but only 26 percent of the reports were received from these areas. Reports of physical abuse from rural areas involved 57 black children and 181 white children.

As shown in Table 6–2, unlike in the state as a whole, reports of abuse in rural areas were received from institutions in roughly equal proportions for black and white children. Relatives reported

more physical abuse of white children than of black children;
in fact, just one black mother made a report. It is interesting
that mothers in general were responsible for so few reports. When
white mothers reported abuse, they reported their sons just
slightly more often than their daughters. These white mothers reported the child's father in 61 percent of the reports and the stepfather in just under 25 percent.

Table 6–2

Percentages of Sources of Reports of Physical Abuse in Rural Areas
by Race * of Victim

Reporting Source	Black (N=57)		White (N=181)	
Relative	21.2		34.4	
Mother		1.8		12.7
Father		1.8		1.7
Grandparent		5.3		9.4
Uncle		1.8		0.6
Aunt		10.5		6.1
Sibling		—		1.1
Stepparent		—		2.8
Institution	26.3		27.2	
Police		1.8		3.9
Sheriff		3.5		0.6
Social worker		—		7.2
School		14.0		9.4
Physician		3.5		2.8
Hospital		3.5		3.3
Other	36.9		21.6	
Friends/neighbors		31.6		16.6
Other**		5.3		5.0
Anonymous	7.0		13.8	
Self	8.8		3.3	

* X^2=10.89; df=4; p=.03

** includes landlords, shopkeepers, employers, babysitters, etc.

The most notable difference between reports of black and white physical abuse was the percentage of reports from friends and neighbors. Almost a third of reports of black physical abuse were received from friends and neighbors; the figure for whites was only 17 percent. Reports from these sources constituted over one-fourth of all the reports of abused black boys and over one-third of the reports of black girls. When friends and neighbors reported black abuse, they overwhelmingly reported abusive mothers; in fact, they reported 44 percent of cases involving abuse by a mother. Neighbors and friends were clearly not as vigilant, or not as willing to report, white children; they accounted for less than one-fifth of the reports for boys and girls (20 and 13 percent, respectively). These reports overwhelmingly targeted parental abuse; over half of the reports targeted a mother and/or a father, while another 30 percent of their reports involved abuse by both parents.

Although the age of the victim was not significantly related to the type of reporter, several interesting patterns emerged. Abuse of black children under the age of ten was reported by "others" 43 percent of the time; these were nonrelative, nonprofessional sources of reports. They included, for example, friends, neighbors, landlords, shopkeepers, babysitters, and so forth. The fact that almost half the abuse was reported by these people, who are likely to be less frequent witnesses than family members, is startling and suggests that other reporting groups were either not "seeing" the abuse or were unwilling to make reports.

Among white children, this same group reported only one-fourth of the abuse of children under five years of age and 18 percent of the abuse of children from five to nine years old. As the age of white victims increased, their relatives reported the abuse in steadily increasing proportions: 31 percent of the reports of children under five, 37 percent of ages five to nine, 42 percent of children aged ten to fourteen, and 41 percent of teenagers fifteen and older. One wonders whether the abuse had been ongoing for some time and the relative's tolerance was finally exceeded, or whether the abuse actually began to occur at that point in the child's life.

Towns and small cities outside of urbanized areas represent sociological characteristics somewhat different from either rural or urban settings. The towns and cities included here have populations of between 10,000 and 50,000 but do not geographically fringe any large metropolitan center. In other words, they might be the center of commerce and service resources for the region, but they do not have the population or multiple industries of urban centers such as Birmingham. Only 6.1 percent of Alabama's black population under age eighteen and 5.5 percent of Alabama's white

Table 6–3

Percentages of Sources of Reports of Physical Abuse in Towns and Small Cities by Race* of Victim

Reporting Source	Black (N=39)		White (N=67)	
Relative	28.2		28.4	
Mother		17.9		16.4
Father		7.7		3.0
Grandparent		2.6		6.0
Uncle		—		1.5
Aunt		—		1.5
Institution	46.2		37.3	
Police		7.7		9.0
Sheriff		—		—
Clergy		2.6		1.5
Social worker		7.7		4.5
School		17.9		11.9
Physician		2.6		4.5
Hospital		7.7		6.0
Other	—		19.4	
Friends/neighbors		—		10.4
Other**		—		9.0
Anonymous	23.1		6.0	
Self	2.6		9.0	

* X^2=15.45; df=4; p=.003
** includes landlords, shopkeepers, employers, babysitters, etc.

population under age eighteen live in these communities. However, as will be discussed in chapter 8, 17 percent of the state's black physical abuse and 19 percent of the state's white physical abuse were reported from these areas. The sources of reports of abuse in towns and small cities are shown in Table 6–3.

White physical abuse was reported in these areas somewhat more often by institutions than by relatives, a reversal of the pattern found in rural areas. Black abuse was reported by institutions almost half of the time, nearly doubling the amount reported by rural institutions; almost one-fifth of all black abuse was reported by schools, and a startling 77 percent of those reports involved victimization of boys.

It is especially interesting that "anonymous" reporters accounted for almost one-fourth of black confirmed abuse but only 6 percent of white confirmed abuse; furthermore, not one report came from the friends and neighbors of black children, the category that contributed the largest proportion of reports in rural areas.

Black relatives in these small communities made more frequent reports of infants (50 percent) than of any other age group, whereas 50 percent of institutional reports of blacks were for preadolescent children (five to nine years old). Unlike the straight linear increase in rural areas, reporting by relatives of white children had a curvilinear relationship with the age of the child, rising to a peak of 47 percent in elementary school years and dropping to 16 percent in late adolescence; institutional reports followed the same curvilinear pattern.

The mothers of both black and white children equally reported physical abuse, a huge increase for black mothers over their rural reporting. When white mothers reported, over 64 percent of the time it was the child's father or stepfather who was abusing, and in 73 percent of reports by a white mother, her son was being abused. When black mothers reported, the father was the perpetrator 44 percent of the time, but in 71 percent of their reports, a daughter was the victim of abuse. In other words, all mothers reported the child's father in a substantial number of cases, but there was a marked racial difference in the sex of the child who was focus of the mother's concerns.

When black mothers committed the abuse, educators reported 26 percent of the time and anonymous reporters, or "unknowns," reported 33 percent. Only one black child made the report herself; she was abused by her mother. Six white children reported their own abuse, and four of these were abused by their stepfathers. Fathers rarely made reports, regardless of race.

A city or urbanized area comprises an incorporated place and, unlike the rural and small-town areas mentioned above, a densely populated surrounding area. Fifty-five percent of Alabama's black population under age eighteen and 42 percent of Alabama's white population under age eighteen live in such urbanized areas. The people who live in urbanized areas are likely to have cultural values, traditions, and expectations, as well as daily routines, markedly different than people living in areas removed from the city. Although they live closer to one another, they can, in fact, live more anonymously. One would expect these differences to contribute to a unique picture of the surveillance, reporting, and caseworker determination of abuse.

The sources of reports from urbanized areas are shown in Table 6–4. Institutions made almost half of all reports of black abuse, just slightly more than the proportion in midsized communities and nearly twice the proportion in rural areas. Institutions made approximately one-third of the reports of white children, the pattern repeated in all community types. Schools represented one-fourth of all reports of black children but only 10 percent of the reports of white children, widening the gap seen in other areas. Hospital reports increased considerably for both blacks and whites, the former almost doubling and the latter more than doubling the proportion of reports from hospitals in towns and small cities. Just two reports of white children and one report of a black child were made by urban physicians.

Relatives made one-fifth of the reports of black and white abuse, with aunts of the child outnumbering mothers, fathers, stepparents, and grandparents in the frequency of black reports. Friends and neighbors made few reports in urban areas, especially of blacks, suggesting an indifference or apathy perhaps unique to urban places.

In white abuse, relatives appeared to be most vigilant toward,

Table 6-4

Percentages of Sources of Reports of Physical Abuse in Urbanized
Areas by Race* of Victim

Reporting Source	Black (N=128)		White (N=98)	
Relative	22.7		20.4	
Mother		5.5		6.1
Father		3.1		4.1
Grandparent		4.7		5.1
Uncle		—		1.0
Aunt		8.6		3.1
Sibling		.8		—
Stepparent		—		1.0
Institution	48.5		35.7	
Police		.8		4.1
Sheriff		1.6		1.0
Clergy		—		1.0
Social worker		8.6		3.1
School		24.2		10.2
Physician		.8		2.0
Hospital		12.5		14.3
Other	11.7		24.5	
Friends/neighbors		8.6		16.3
Other**		3.1		8.2
Anonymous	11.7		13.3	
Self	5.5		6.1	

* $X^2 = 7.99$; df=4; NS
** includes landlords, shopkeepers, employers, babysitters, etc.

or willing to report, abuse of children between infancy and elementary school age (five to nine years old); only 25 percent of all
relative-initiated reports involved children older than ten. This
trend is not true of black relatives, who made the bulk of their
reports (38 percent) concerning children ten to fourteen years old.

Institutional reports were more consistent across age groups, with reports decreasing only in the later adolescent years (as they do for all reporting sources) for both blacks and whites. It is interesting that both black and white children reported themselves as victims of abuse as young as the elementary school age group. Girls of both races reported themselves five times more often than boys.

When the mother was the confirmed perpetrator of black abuse, almost one-quarter of all reports originated with the school system. In all, 42 percent were professional/institutional reports. Ranked second to schools, aunts were an unexpected source of reports of abuse perpetrated by the mother. When a white mother was accused of abuse, the school system was the modal source of reports, as it was with black mothers (25 and 24 percent, respectively). Both black and white fathers made only four reports each. It is interesting that of the few children who made the report themselves (seven blacks, six whites), half of the white children reported being abused by a stepmother, and these were the only cases of stepmother-perpetrated abuse.

When the father was the declared perpetrator, which occurred in only 15 percent of black abuse, hospitals and schools together accounted for half of the reports and the child's mother accounted for another 20 percent. In white urban families, on the other hand, the mother reported the child's father in less than 10 percent of father-perpetrated abuse. In fact, when a white father was accused of abuse, reports were more often made by a friend or neighbor (29 percent) than by any other source, although anonymous reporters were a close second (27 percent).

SUMMARY

This investigation into the incidence of child abuse reporting supports in part the hypothesized influence of cultural and community differences. The sources of physical abuse reports varied considerably with the size of the community. Only in urban areas was the relationship between sources of reports and race not significant. Although it was predicted that the source of reports and community size would be significantly related for both races, this was true only for reporting sources of black children.

If there were no community patterns we would expect the proportion of professional reports, for example, to be approximately equal everywhere. However, as shown in Figure 6–1, institutional reports, which were an important source in all locations, increased considerably for both black and white children between rural and urban communities, and, except in rural areas, these institutional sources consistently reported more black than white children. There is the possibility that the largest communities have more professional and institutional resources and, therefore, the opportunity for a broader surveillance and reporting network. However, many of the professional sources we considered (such as police, sheriff, social worker, physician, schools) are proportionate to the populations they serve. Although it is known that black families more frequently utilize hospital emergency rooms, the greater predominance of school reports of blacks, regardless of community size, cannot be similarly explained. Schools have a wide variety of self-imposed reporting requirements. Some schools allow teachers to make reports directly to DPS; other schools require the teacher to channel the report through the principal's office in order to protect the teacher's identity and thereby safeguard the loss of the teacher's time to a court hearing. The actual effect that these mechanisms have on reliability cannot be unraveled with these data. Several important questions therefore remain unanswered: Are black children actually more frequently abused, or are schools and hospitals exhibiting a racial bias in reporting? Do hospitals and schools have a higher threshold for injury of white children than black children, that is, must the injuries be more severe or visible on white children? Are they simply less willing to risk reporting a white family, or do they deny the existence of white abuse until the injuries are unequivocal? Can these differences be interpreted as an increased concern and vigilance toward black children or, on the other hand, as an opportunity taken to "confirm" a racial prejudice?

Relative reporters, also an active reporting group for both races, were more watchful of white children in rural areas, decreasing their reporting frequency as the size of the community increased. Another nonprofessional source of reports, neighbors and friends, made a substantial number of reports of rural black

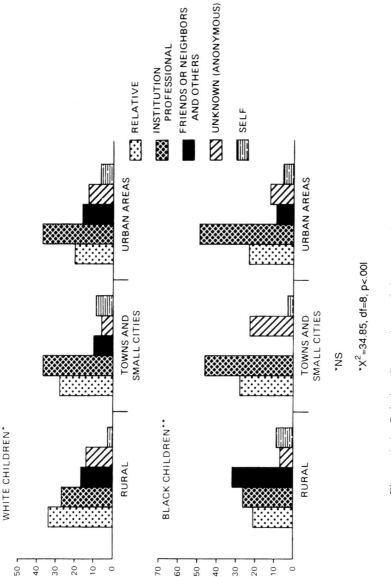

Figure 6–1   Relative Proportions of Sources of Reports of Physical Abuse in Rural, Midsized, and Urbanized Areas

children, but none in midsized communities and few in urban areas. It may be that the large proportion of anonymous reporters in the small communities, where someone choosing not to be identified initiated almost one-fourth of all reports of black children, were in fact friends and neighbors who chose to retain confidentiality even within the system. These data may indicate a concern among reporters (of black children) for their secrecy, or perhaps liability, in these communities, a concern they did not appear to have in more rural areas. There is the additional possibility that black families in small communities, whose extended kin networks are in close proximity, have developed their own internal surveillance and intervention strategies.

A more complete understanding of reporting patterns among these nonrelative and institutional reporting sources is prevented by the fact that reporters are not identified by race. Therefore, we cannot study (as we can with relatives) whether any significant racial patterns occur in either surveillance or reporting by individuals within these groups. In order to strengthen and educate the child abuse surveillance-reporting system, it would be worthwhile to document the reporting sources with the intention of investigating the origins, motivations, and reliability of this reporting network.

Sexual Abuse

THE SOURCES OF REPORTS STATEWIDE

In the twenty-five sample counties, 211 cases of sexual abuse were confirmed. Forty-nine of the cases involved black female victims, 12 cases involved black males, 114 cases involved white females, and 36 cases involved white males; 29 percent of the victims were black, and 71 percent were white. The twenty-eight children who were both physically and sexually abused have been included in these numbers. The five black children (four girls) and six white children (all girls) who were raped were also included in the sexual abuse reports for analysis.

More than one-third of the white sexual abuse reported in Alabama was identified, as shown in Table 6–5, by relatives of the victim, principally the child's mother; relatives reported 24 percent of all black sexual abuse, with the mothers and aunts making the most frequent reports. Interestingly, institutions, such as schools and hospitals, made 40 percent of the reports of confirmed sexual abuse in the state (58 percent of black abuse, but only 33 percent of white abuse).

The most frequent specific source of reports of black sexual

Table 6–5

Statewide Percentages of Sources of Reports of Sexual Abuse by Race[*] of Victim

Reporting Source	Black (N=54)		White (N=138)	
Relative	24.1		36.2	
Mother		14.8		21.5
Father		—		.7
Grandparent		—		4.4
Aunt		7.4		3.7
Sibling		1.9		3.7
Stepparent		—		2.2
Institution	57.6		33.3	
Police		1.9		1.5
Sheriff		1.9		2.2
Clergy		—		.7
Social worker		13.0		7.4
School		3.7		11.1
Physician		5.6		6.7
Hospital		31.5		3.7
Other	5.6		17.1	
Friends/neighbors		3.7		10.4
Other**		1.9		6.7
Anonymous	7.4		4.4	
Self	5.6		8.9	

[*] X^2=11.54; df=4; p=.02

^{**} includes landlords, shopkeepers, employers, babysitters, etc.

abuse were hospitals (32 percent), which made only 4 percent, eight times less, of the reports of white sexual abuse. (Note that this category does not include physicians but may include any other professional employed by a hospital.) Fewer than 8 percent of the reports of both races came directly from the sexually abused victim. When children reported themselves as victims of sexual abuse (as did three blacks and twelve whites), the father was the perpetrator in 50 percent of the cases (60 percent of black reports and 46 percent of white reports). Stepfathers were the perpetrators in an additional 27 percent of white self-reports.

When the father (who was the most prevalent offender) was the perpetrator of white sexual abuse, he was reported by the child's mother 25 percent of the time, by the child 15 percent of the time, and by a social worker 13 percent of the time. Interestingly, black mothers never reported fathers for sexual abuse; in fact, in black abuse, no clear reporting patterns emerged relative to specific perpetrators.

COMPARISON OF COMMUNITY SIZE AND SOURCES OF REPORTS

Only 38 percent of the 211 reports of abuse in 1982 involved children from rural areas. Of these reports, 75 percent involved white victims and 25 percent involved black victims; these figures compared with a rural population under eighteen years of age that is 79 percent white and 20 percent black. The quarter of victims who were black comprised fourteen girls and six boys; there were 47 reports of white girls and 14 reports of white boys. In rural areas, 39 percent of all sexual abuse was reported by relatives of the child, with mothers reporting 21 percent of the total. Institutions reported an additional 36 percent, with 14 percent of the reports by educators and 15 percent by people involved with health care. Ten percent of the reports of sexual abuse were received from the victims themselves.

As shown in Table 6–6, institutions were responsible for half of the reports of black sexual abuse but for just less than a third of the white reports, the difference due principally to the greater number of hospital reports of black children. On the other hand, relatives reported 42 percent of white sexual abuse but only 30 percent of black abuse. Mothers were the reporters in almost a quarter of the reports of white abuse, compared with only 15 percent of the black reports. The proportions of unknown reports, self-reports, and reports by friends and neighbors were relatively equal for both races and, especially for blacks, demonstrate a marked decrease over the proportion of physical abuse reports. When black mothers reported sexual abuse, the victims were always their daughters; reports from white mothers, however, concerned their sons in a surprising 36 percent of the cases. Educators who reported sexual abuse also reported only female victims; they made 28 percent of the reports of abused black girls and

Table 6-6

Percentages of Sources of Reports of Sexual Abuse in Rural Areas by Race* of Victim

Reporting Source	Black	White
Relative	30.0 (N=6)	41.6 (N=25)
Mother	15.0	23.3
Grandparent	—	8.3
Aunt	15.0	5.0
Sibling	—	5.0
Institution	50.0 (N=10)	31.7 (N=19)
Sheriff	—	1.7
Social worker	5.0	6.7
School	20.0	11.7
Physician	10.0	10.0
Hospital	15.0	1.7
Other	5.0 (N=1)	10.0 (N=6)
Friends/neighbors	5.0	3.3
Other**	—	6.7
Anonymous	5.0 (N=1)	6.7 (N=4)
Self	10.0 (N=2)	10.0 (N=6)

* X^2=2.41; df=4; NS
** includes landlords, shopkeepers, employers, babysitters, etc.

less than half that percentage of abuse involving white girls.

As described earlier, only 6.1 percent of Alabama's black population and 5.5 percent of Alabama's white population under age eighteen live in towns and small cities. However, 20 percent (N = 12) of all black and 21 percent (N = 32) of all white sexual abuse confirmed in Alabama took place in these midsized communities. In sexual abuse, unlike physical abuse, the relationship between the source of reports and the race of the child in these communities was not statistically significant; however, relatives reported more white abuse, institutions reported more black abuse, and there were no reports of black abuse from friends or neighbors (see Table 6–7). The majority of reports of white sexual abuse were made by relatives of victims and involved older children; institutions made most of the remaining reports. Black children were reported equally by relatives (mostly aunts) and institutions; three children (27 percent) reported themselves. White mothers accounted for 38 percent of the reports of sexual abuse, while black mothers made only 9 percent, a much greater difference than that found in rural areas. Hospitals made twice as many reports of black abuse as did black mothers but, interestingly, reported no confirmed white sexual abuse. Overall, white sexual abuse was reported by a wider variety of sources than black abuse.

No discernible pattern occurred between reporters and perpetrators in black sexual abuse, as was found in rural areas. In white sexual abuse, on the other hand, mothers, stepmothers, and the girls themselves each reported 25 percent of father-perpetrated abuse. Only one report was made by a white father; it was a case of white sexual abuse, and the accused was the mother's boyfriend. One black mother reported the sexual abuse of her daughter by her stepfather. Social workers appeared most alert to sexual abuse perpetrated by white stepfathers.

The total number of children confirmed as having been sexually abused in urbanized areas was small: twenty-two black children, one of whom was a boy, and forty-four white children, ten of whom were boys. In urbanized areas, black sexual abuse was reported almost entirely by institutions (71 percent), and 52 percent of black reports came from hospitals (see Table 6–8). The fre-

Table 6–7

Percentages of Sources of Reports of Sexual Abuse in Towns and Small
Cities by Race* of Victim

Reporting Source	Black	White
Relative	36.4 (N=4)	53.1 (N=17)
Mother	9.1	37.5
Father	—	3.1
Grandparent	—	6.3
Aunt	27.3	3.1
Stepparent	—	3.1
Institution	36.4 (N=4)	25.0 (N=8)
Police	—	3.1
Sheriff	9.1	3.1
Clergy	—	3.1
Social worker	9.1	9.4
School	—	3.1
Physician	—	3.1
Hospital	18.2	—
Other	—	15.6 (N=5)
Friends/neighbors	—	12.5
Other**	—	3.1
Self	27.3 (N=3)	6.3 (N=2)

* X^2=5.67; df=3; NS

** includes landlords, shopkeepers, employers, babysitters, etc.

quency of institutional reports of blacks was consistent across age
groups. In comparison, institutions reported slightly more than a
third of white sexual abuse, but schools, which reported no black
sexual abuse, outnumbered hospitals in the number of reports of
white abuse.

All reports by relatives were of girls, three-fourths of whom
were between ten and fourteen years old. When a white child's
father was the perpetrator of abuse, almost one-third of the reports were made by the child's mother; when these white mothers

Table 6-8

Percentages of Sources of Reports of Sexual Abuse in Urbanized
Areas by Race * of Victim

Reporting Source	Black	White
Relative	23.8 (N=5)	26.2 (N=11)
Mother	19.0	16.7
Aunt	—	2.4
Sibling	4.8	7.1
Institution	71.4 (N=15)	38.1 (N=16)
Police	4.8	—
Sheriff	—	2.4
Social worker	14.3	7.1
School	—	14.3
Physician	—	2.4
Hospital	52.4	11.9
Other	—	26.2 (N=11)
Friends/neighbors	—	16.7
Other**	—	9.5
Anonymous	4.8 (N=1)	2.4 (N=1)
Self	—	7.1 (N=3)

* X^2=10.93; df=4; p=.03
** includes landlords, shopkeepers, employers, babysitters, etc.

reported abuse, they reported the father almost two-thirds of the
time. Only one report of both parents abusing the child did not
come from friends and neighbors. No other discernible patterns
of reporting occurred with respect to race of the victim or the
perpetrator of abuse.

SUMMARY

The sources of reports of sexual abuse were not as strongly
related to community size as was true of physical abuse reporting

sources. Relatives and other nonprofessionals were active reporters of both physically and sexually abused children, regardless of
location. Especially in towns and small cities, relatives accounted
for the majority of reports of sexual abuse of white children. Hospitals, however, rarely reported sexual abuse of white children;
only one white child outside of an urbanized area was reported by
a hospital. It is hard to explain the high proportion of hospital
reports and the low incidence of injury among black children in
urban areas (see chapter 8), and it would be interesting to know
what clues prompted hospital suspicion of abuse. Although urban
white children were injured more often, they were referred by
hospitals infrequently, and in only one instance by a physician.
Hospitals appear more willing to report and/or to suspect black
abuse; white children, injured or not, did not get reported.

The relationships between community size, race, and sources
of reports are complex. Significant racial differences occurred in
physical abuse reporting sources in both rural and midsized communities but not in urban communities; urban areas, however,
were the only locations in which statistically significant racial differences occurred in sexual abuse reporting. In addition, only
among blacks was there an overall statistically significant relationship between reporting sources and community size and then
only in physical abuse.

The differences in reporting sources therefore appear to be
greater between races than between communities. In only two instances were physical and sexual abuse reporting sources significantly different within race; significant differences were found
only in rural white abuse reports and in black abuse reports from
towns and small cities. In other words, the reporting patterns
were roughly equivalent whether the report concerned black sexual abuse or black physical abuse; the same holds true for reporting sources of abused white children.

Statistical significance is affected by cell size, and in sexual
abuse the numbers are very small. However, using Figures 6–1
and 6–2 as guides, rather than relying upon statistical tests alone,
the differences between communities appear quite dramatic. Several of these relationships have been discussed above, such as the
absence of physical abuse reports of black children in midsized

70

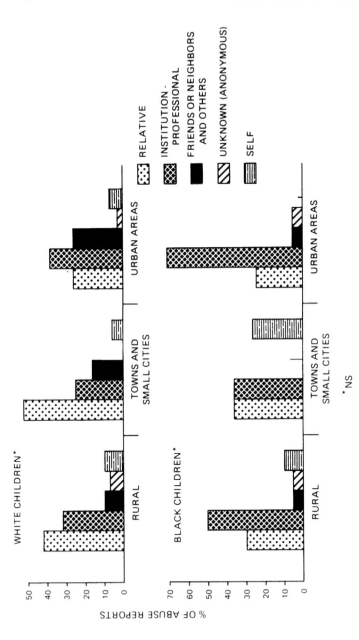

Figure 6–2 Relative Proportions of Sources of Reports of Sexual Abuse
in Rural, Midsized, and Urbanized Areas

communities from friends and neighbors, the most prevalent rural source of reports. Friends and neighbors also made no reports of sexually abused black children in communities outside of rural areas.

All in all, friends and neighbors were more frequent reporters of white abuse, relatives were consistent reporters in both races and in all communities, and institutions made reports of black children with far greater frequency. Institutions, as expected, and in fact as mandated by law, were significant contributors to the total numbers of reports.

7
Results of the Study: The State

This chapter presents physical and sexual abuse research findings in the state as a whole. These statewide results are included for two reasons: (1) to allow comparison to other epidemiological reports, and (2) to illustrate the importance of the three distinct geopolitical units—rural places, towns or small cities, and urbanized areas—to an understanding of the context of child abuse.

As shown in Figure 7–1, 6,866 children were reported as abused or neglected in the twenty-five sample counties in fiscal year 1982, representing a rate of 13.31 children under age eighteen per 1,000 in the population. Reports were incomplete on 81 children; in other words, DPS Form 959 gave no indication whether these children were reported as neglected or abused, and no narratives were attached. Of the remaining children, almost two-thirds were reported as neglected; 39 percent of these reports were confirmed by the investigator, yielding a founded neglect rate of 3.32. Forty-four percent of the reports of neglected children were determined by the investigator to be unfounded allegations (see Table 7–1), representing a significant contribution of caseworkers' time to investigations of false allegations.

There were 2,376 children reported as abused; 160 of these reports were incomplete. Over three-fourths of these children were reported as physically abused, with confirmation at 34 percent. Of the 421 reports of sexually abused children, just over 200 were declared founded, a confirmation rate of 50 percent. Only 9 percent of the total number of reports to the system were confirmed as physical abuse and 3 percent confirmed as sexual abuse. These figures indicate that, following the caseworkers' investigations, two-thirds of all reports to the system were considered to be

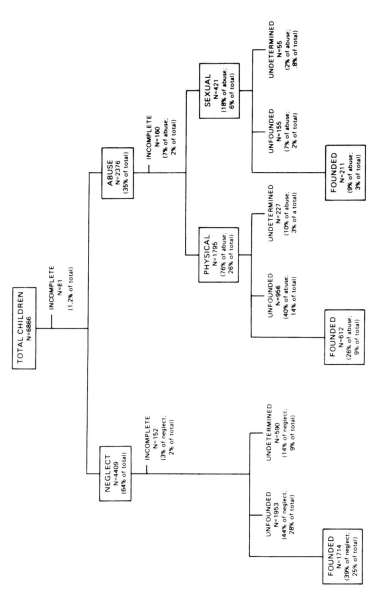

Figure 7–1 Percentages of Founded, Unfounded, and Undetermined Reports of Abuse and Neglect

Table 7-1

Determinations on 1982 Alabama Central Registry Reports for
Twenty-five Sample Counties

Determination	Neglect (N=4,409)	Physical Abuse (N=1,795)	Sexual Abuse (N=421)
Incomplete	3%	*	*
Confirmed	39%	34%	50%
Unfounded	44%	53%	37%
Undetermined	14%	13%	13%
	100%	100%	100%

*
Abuse reports that were incomplete could not be separated into
physical and sexual abuse categories (7 percent of abuse reports).

falsely reported, good news with respect to the final numbers of
children abused and neglected in Alabama. Nonetheless, each
child who is reported must be assumed to be abused or neglected
prior to a thorough investigation and the elimination of all doubt
as to the child's danger. The final numbers, then, do not reflect the
amount of time and effort contributed to the investigation. However, it can be hypothesized that the time the caseworker spends
in the investigation of these falsely reported cases—time spent
with the child and his or her family—contributes significantly to
the education of families about prevention of abuse or neglect.

This research was designed to investigate confirmed abuse and
its characteristics. Therefore, the study population in the following analyses includes the 823 children whose reports of physical
or sexual abuse were confirmed. As shown in Table 7-2, only
twelve cases of emotional abuse were confirmed. Due to the small
number, no further analyses included these children. Twenty-

Table 7–2

Statewide Confirmed Abuse by Type of Abuse, Race, and Sex of Victim

Type of Abuse	Black N (%)	White N (%)	Total N (%)
Physical Abuse	233(78.7)	379(70.3)	612(73.3)
Male	117(39.5)	211(39.1)	328(39.3)
Female	116(39.2)	168(31.2)	284(34.0)
Sexual Abuse*	61(20.6)	150(27.8)	211(25.2)
Male	12(4.0)	36(6.7)	48(5.7)
Female	49(16.6)	114(21.1)	163(19.5)
Emotional Abuse	2(.7)	10(1.9)	12(1.4)
Male	—	(.6)	3(.4)
Female	2(.7)	7(1.3)	9(1.0)
	296(35.4)	539(64.6)	835(100.0)

*
includes both rape (N=11) and combined physical and sexual abuse (N=28).

eight children, including 12 blacks (11 females) and 16 whites (11 females), were both sexually and physically abused and 11 children (6 white girls, 4 black girls, and 1 black boy) were raped. These incidents were added to the sexual abuse total for analysis.

The rates of sexual and physical abuse in the twenty-five sampled counties are presented in Table 7–3. The highest rate of physical abuse was in Shelby County (2.56 children under age eighteen per 1,000 in the population); the lowest rate, .48, was in Autauga County. (Note that DeKalb County had a 32 percent incomplete rate and, therefore, those results are considered unreliable.)

Table 7-3

1982 Confirmed Physical and Sexual Abuse Rates in Sample Counties

County	Population under 18	Physical N	Physical Rate	Sexual N	Sexual Rate
Autauga	12,400	6	.48	5	.40
Calhoun	41,410	87	2.10	29	.70
Cherokee	6,160	6	.97	8	1.30
Choctaw	5,990	8	1.33	5	.83
Clarke	9,820	6	.61	1	.10
Clay	4,670	6	1.28	—	.00
Cleburne	4,180	7	1.67	—	.00
Colbert	17,850	11	.62	4	.22
Coosa *	3,820	7	1.83*	—	.00*
DeKalb	18,160	6	.33	1	.06
Escambia	12,760	29	2.27	6	.47
Fayette	6,290	11	1.75	4	.64
Franklin	9,130	16	1.75	—	.00
Geneva	8,340	11	1.32	5	.60
Greene	4,410	4	.90	5	1.13
Hale	5,940	6	1.01	3	.51
Jackson	16,660	10	.60	14	.84
Jefferson	207,350	154	.74	64	.31
Perry	5,920	6	1.01	3	.51
Pike	9,870	22	2.23	5	.51
Russell	16,380	41	2.50	18	1.10
Shelby	14,440	37	2.56	8	.55
Talladega	20,220	37	1.82	10	.49
Tuscaloosa	47,080	69	1.47	11	.23
Washington	6,570	9	1.36	2	.30
		612		211	

*
Thirty-two percent of the reports were incomplete; the rates of
abuse, therefore, are unreliable.

Physical Abuse in the State

THE VICTIMS

Surprisingly, roughly 30 percent of black and 34 percent of white physical abuse took place in families with just one child. Black and white families with two children accounted for 25 and 31 percent, respectively. The average number of children in the home was 2.52 for blacks, 2.19 for whites, with a range of 1 to 8 for blacks and 1 to 7 for whites. In both black and white reports, only 1 child was confirmed as abused in 80 percent of the investigations. Two children were abused in under 15 percent of the reports. The total number of children abused per report ranged from 1 to 6.

White children represented almost two-thirds (62 percent) of all confirmed physical abuse. Because whites constituted three-fourths of Alabama's population, however, the rates of abuse, which are shown in Table 7–4, were higher among blacks than among whites (1.29 versus 1.07). Both black boys and black girls had approximately the same physical abuse rates; white boys, however, had rates considerably higher than white girls, although their rates never reached the magnitude of blacks of either sex.

Table 7–4

Statewide Physical Abuse Rates* by Race and Sex of Victim

Sex	Black (N=233)	White (N=379)
Male	1.27	1.15
Female	1.29	.98
Total	1.28	1.07

* $\dfrac{\text{\# abused}}{\text{population under 18}} \times 1000$

AGE OF THE VICTIMS

It is interesting that among infants, white boys and black girls had a 20 percent higher rate of physical abuse than either black boys or white girls, as shown in Table 7–5. In the group of children aged five to nine, the risk for black males increased by 66 percent to an outstanding rate of 2.08 per 1,000, whereas no other groups showed any increase at all. This huge increase may have been due to the greater prevalence of school system reports of black children, although this does not explain why boys are reported with greater frequency than girls. Physical abuse rates were higher among black children than white children in the group of children aged ten to fourteen, but they dipped significantly for both races in the adolescent group. White physical abuse was consistently greater for boys than for girls from birth to age fourteen (see Figure 7–2). The dramatic fall in abuse rates among children older than fifteen was probably due in part to their greater physical size and strength (and thus their greater capacity to defend themselves or to retaliate) and in part to the reporters' assuming the children sufficiently mature to take care of themselves, that is, as old enough to do their own protecting or reporting.

SMSA VERSUS NON-SMSA OR "RURAL" VERSUS "URBAN" ABUSE

As described previously, the SMSA, or standard metropolitan statistical area, is a statistical standard developed for use by

Table 7–5

Statewide Rates of Physical Abuse by Age, Race, and Sex of Victim

Age	Black (N=233)		White (N=379)	
	Male	Female	Male	Female
0 – 4	1.25	1.54	1.52	1.24
5 – 9	2.08	1.38	1.39	1.24
10 – 14	1.54	1.46	1.24	.85
15 – 18	.28	.85	.58	.70

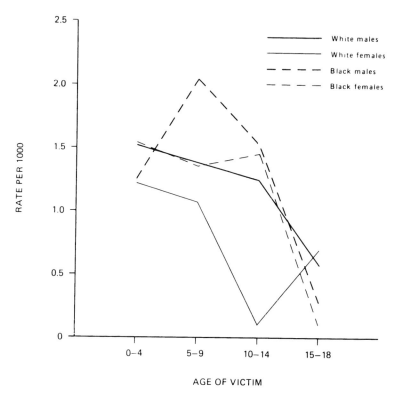

Figure 7–2   Rates of Physical Abuse in Alabama

federal agencies in the production, analysis, and publication of data on metropolitan areas, as defined by the U.S. Office of Management and Budget. It is misleading to use the SMSA when trying to sort out the socioeconomic, or even geographic, factors in urban and rural living with the occurrence of child abuse. Nonetheless, the SMSA/non-SMSA rates of child abuse are reported here for comparison with other epidemiological studies that have utilized SMSA population figures to calculate "urban" abuse and non-SMSA area figures to calculate "rural" abuse. The following sections of this chapter, however, will also divide Alabama's population into more conceptually meaningful rural, midsized, and urban units.

Table 7–6 shows the rates of physical abuse by the race, sex, and age of the child as well as by the SMSA/non-SMSA designation. As can be seen, blacks in general had higher rates in SMSA areas, although the rates were more dramatic among black

Table 7–6

Rates of Physical Abuse in SMSA/Non-SMSA by Race, Sex, and Age of Victim

Victim	Age	SMSA	Non-SMSA
Black male		1.27	1.26
	0 – 4	1.44	.78
	5 – 9	1.82	2.65
	10 – 14	1.64	1.30
	15 – 18	.28	.29
Black female		1.43	.99
	0 – 4	1.64	1.35
	5 – 9	1.56	.93
	10 – 14	1.60	1.11
	15 – 18	.98	.54
White male		1.04	1.39
	0 – 4	1.37	1.84
	5 – 9	1.11	2.00
	10 – 14	1.20	1.31
	15 – 18	.59	.54
White female		.91	1.11
	0 – 4	1.19	1.33
	5 – 9	1.23	1.17
	10 – 14	.75	1.04
	15 – 18	.58	.94

females. White children, on the other hand, had higher rates of physical abuse in the nonmetropolitan areas. Whether this difference was a function of reporter bias, caseworker bias, or true abuse incidence is obviously an important issue but one that would be extremely hard to unravel. Black children typically had higher rates in metropolitan areas, except for those children between the ages of five and nine who had a higher rate in non-SMSA areas; in fact, these rates were the highest rates of physical abuse of any group in the state.

THE CONTEXT OF ABUSE

Four-fifths of all physical abuse occurred in the home of the child, whether black or white. Abuse was also noted, though very low in frequencies, in relatives' and neighbors' homes, in schools, outdoors, in public places such as movie theaters and churches, and even in hospitals. In both black and white abuse, the modal household included four to five persons; the number of black children ranged from one to nine with roughly equivalent (20 percent) proportions having one, two, and three children. In white households, 32 percent had two children; equal proportions (22 percent) had one to three, with a range of one to seven. The relationship between race and the number of children per household was statistically significant ($X^2 = 21.10$; df = 9; p = .01).

The household situation in which the child lived obviously determined, at least in part, who was present to commit the abuse. In other words, children living in female-headed households were less likely to be abused by their fathers and, likewise, children living in a foster home had less likelihood of being abused by either parent. As a result, the perpetrators of abuse and the types of households in which abuse occurred were highly interrelated. It is necessary, therefore, to take into account the proportions of the various types of households within which black and white children lived within the state as a whole in order to interpret both the risk associated with household type and the risk associated with a particular perpetrator of abuse. This step, in effect, is equivalent to calculating rates by controlling, not for the size of the population at risk (as above), but for the frequency of occurrence of household types in the population at large.

In 1982 in the state of Alabama, 35 percent of black children and 10 percent of white children lived in homes in which a female was designated as the head of household. In our sample of confirmed cases of child abuse, 55 percent of the physically abused black children lived in female-headed households. White children, on the other hand, lived in female-headed households in 19 percent of the physical abuse cases (see Table 7–7). However, comparing these percentages to the statewide proportions of household type reverses what appeared to be a greater risk among black children: calculating a risk ratio by dividing the rate for this subset by the rate for the entire state resulted in 2.1 for whites, considerably higher than the risk ratio of 1.5 for blacks.

Table 7–7

Statewide Percentages of Physical Abuse by Type of Household, Race,[*] and Sex of Victim

Household Type	Black			White		
	Male (N=109)[vs.]	Female (N=114)	% Total Abuse	Male (N=200)[vs.]	Female (N=155)	% Total Abuse
Female– headed	45.5	54.4	55.2	46.4	53.6	19.4
Both biological parents	50.0	50.0	19.7	55.1	44.9	41.4
Father only	66.7	33.3	1.3	47.1	52.9	4.8
Stepfamily	51.5	48.5	14.8	67.0	33.0	31.5
Other[**]	56.2	43.8	9.0	40.0	60.0	2.9

[*] $X^2=106.42$; df=8; p=.00

[**] refers to households in which a foster parent, an adoptive parent, a grandparent, a sibling, or an unknown person is the household head

Any number of factors may contribute to the higher risk for white children. In Alabama, white mothers living as household heads were more likely than black mothers to be divorced; our data bear this out: 44 percent of the white mothers heading their own households were divorced women, while only 13 percent of black mothers were divorced. Almost 30 percent of black mothers had never been married, and the marital status of another 30 percent was declared by the caseworker as unknown. Fewer than 5 percent of white mothers had never been married. Not surprisingly, the relationship between marital status and race of female heads of households is statistically significant ($X^2 = 40.28$; $df = 12$; $p = .00$). These figures suggest a heightened surveillance of mothers who lived without a male designated as head of household.

Both black and white girls were abused somewhat more frequently in households headed by women than were boys (54 to 46 percent). It is noteworthy that mothers perpetrated the abuse of their children in almost three-fourths of the black households they headed. In white female-headed households, mothers were the perpetrators in only 58 percent of the reports, and the male friends of the mother were responsible for the greatest percentage of the remaining abuse (17 percent). Inasmuch as there is no reason to assume that more female children live in homes headed by women, the evidence of a greater risk of abuse is likely to be associated with a problematic mother-daughter relationship. In these households, it may be that the sons assumed (or were assigned) the role of male head and were therefore protected from abuse. In white homes with both parents present, on the other hand, sons were victimized over daughters 55 to 45 percent and in stepfamilies, 67 to 33 percent. Black boys and girls were equally victimized when they lived with both biological parents or with stepparents.

Unfortunately, numbers of children living in two-parent households are collected by the Bureau of the Census without distinguishing between biological parents and stepparents. As a result, it is not possible to calculate similar risk ratios for these groups.

The vast majority of abuse was perpetrated by the victim's

Table 7-8

Statewide Percentages of Perpetrators of Physical Abuse by Race and Sex of Victim

	Black			White		
Perpetrator	Male (N=112) vs.	Female (N=114)	% Total Abuse	Male (N=200) vs.	Female (N=156)	% Total Abuse
Father	55.6	44.4	15.9	59.3	40.7	33.1
Mother	47.5	52.5	52.2	51.0	49.0	27.0
Both biological parents	27.3	72.7	4.9	42.9	57.1	9.8
Stepfather	46.7	53.3	6.6	71.4	28.6	13.8
Stepmother	20.0	80.0	2.2	51.0	49.0	3.7
Grandfather	100.0	—	.4	68.0	32.0	.8
Grandmother	75.0	25.0	3.5	25.0	75.0	1.1
Uncle	50.0	50.0	1.8	—	100.0	.3
Aunt	60.0	40.0	2.2	—	100.0	.3
Brother	—	100.0	.4	—	100.0	.8
Male friend	42.9	57.1	3.1	50.0	50.5	5.1
Female friend	50.0	50.0	.9	—	—	—
Other*	69.0	31.0	5.6	78.8	21.2	4.3

*
 includes babysitter, foster parent, adoptive parent, foster
 sibling, brother-in-law, stepsibling, cousin, and unidentified
 perpetrator

caretaker (an adult with whom the child lived). In black physical abuse of both boys and girls, for example, over 80 percent was perpetrated by a caretaker, 9 percent was perpetrated by a non-caretaker relative, and the remaining was abuse by "outsiders." Similarly, almost 90 percent of white physical abuse was perpetrated by a caretaker and less than 4 percent by a noncaretaker relative. These figures are obviously related to the fact that caretakers spend the greatest amount of time with the child, thereby increasing the opportunity for abusive incidents to develop. Abuse by a regular member of the child's household may also represent a more serious matter to a potential reporter than what might be considered an unusual fit of anger by someone who is not a household member.

The age of the perpetrators was recorded in less than half the reports, but it can be speculated from the high occurrence of families in which there was only one child that the perpetrators were relatively young. The perpetrators of physical abuse are shown in Table 7–8. White male children were clearly at greater risk when a father or father figure was present. For example, when fathers and stepfathers abused, they struck out at their sons over daughters in an overwhelming majority of cases (59 and 71 percent respectively). It is interesting that within black families, fathers abused their sons (56 percent) but stepfathers abused their daughters (53 percent) more often. In both races, when the mother and father were both confirmed abusers, their daughters were victimized far more often than their sons (73 percent in black families; 57 percent in white families).

THE INJURIES RESULTING FROM ABUSE

The more severe injuries, such as fractures and burns, were not reported by institutions; over three-fourths of the reports of fractured bones and four-fifths of the reports of burns were from nonprofessional sources. The few reports made by physicians involved psychological damage more often than physical; all but one of these cases were white children. Most children with bruises were reported by relatives, except for white girls, whose bruises were identified more often by professionals. As shown in Table 7–9, bruises were noted on more than three-fourths of both black and white children. Black children suffered cuts and abrasions almost twice as often as white children.

Approximately one-fourth of the black children were medically examined, the girls considerably more often than the boys (59 to 41 percent). A slightly smaller proportion of medical examinations occurred among white children, with boys receiving care somewhat more often than girls (55 to 45 percent). Of the black children who received medical attention for their abuse-related injuries, 28 percent were reported by hospitals and 4 percent were reported by physicians. Among medically evaluated white children, 9 percent were reported by physicians and 27 percent by hospitals. The remaining reports originated outside the medical setting. In

Table 7-9

Statewide Percentages of Children Receiving Injury in Physical Abuse by Type of Injury, Race, and Sex of Victim

	Black			White		
Injury	Male (N=112) vs.	Female (N=114)	% Total Abuse*	Male (N=200) vs.	Female (N=156)	% Total Abuse*
No injury	65.5	34.5	12.8	60.0	40.0	12.6
Bruises	49.1	50.9	77.4	55.3	44.7	76.1
Burns	62.5	37.5	3.5	50.0	50.0	1.1
Cuts	45.4	54.6	24.3	63.8	36.2	13.2
Death	—	100.0	.9	—	—	—
Fractures	46.1	53.9	5.8	66.7	33.3	5.1
Neurological	50.0	50.0	1.8	25.0	75.0	1.1
Psychological effects	26.6	73.4	13.3	64.1	35.9	18.8

*Because some children received multiple injuries, the columns add to more than 100 percent

other words, 68 percent of the black injured children and 64 percent of the white injured children were treated medically, but no report was made by medical professionals.

An interesting finding, although dependent on the narrative style and content of the investigative report, was the mention of psychological injury in only 19 percent of white physical abuse and 13 percent of black physical abuse. It may well be, of course, that caseworkers consider psychological damage to be understood and therefore not to require notation.

Infant boys and girls of both races received bruises most frequently; cuts became more frequent as the age of the child increased. In general, the older the child, the more often a notable injury had occurred; for example, only two white males and four white females over age fifteen had no visible injury, and there were no teenage black children without injuries. One could assume that visible injury serves as a criterion for reporting and/or confirmation of physical abuse among these adolescent children.

Although data were not collected on weapons or other means of inflicting injury, the research team members were polled as to their individual recall of those reports in which such means were mentioned; their impressions ranked the hand or fist as the most frequently used weapon, with belts and electrical extension cords in a close tie for second.

DISPOSITION OF CASES

The data on the disposition of cases were scant. Although required by the reporting law, a large number of caseworker narrative reports gave no details about the follow-through of cases, due certainly to the thirty-day deadline for submitting the investigation summary. Therefore, although the reports may have failed to include information, it cannot be assumed that services were not rendered. The most accurate of the disposition findings, in which fewer than 5 percent of the reports were missing information, concerned the removal or retention in the home of the victim of abuse. In a surprising third of the cases of physical abuse, the child was at least temporarily removed from his or her household. Blacks were put into foster care somewhat more often than whites

(16 to 10 percent), and white children were placed into the homes of their relatives somewhat more often than were black children (12 to 9 percent). These differences were not, however, statistically significant.

In very rare instances was the perpetrator arrested or charged criminally: eleven black cases (five fathers, four mothers, an aunt, and a teacher) and twenty-four white cases (thirteen fathers, three mothers, four male friends of the mother, one stepfather, one grandfather, one brother, and one case in which both parents were charged). The perpetrator was removed from the household in fourteen black incidents; five were fathers, five were stepfathers, two were mothers, one was an uncle, and, in one instance, both parents were removed. Among the thirty-two white abuse cases in which the perpetrator was removed, fathers accounted for 56 percent of the total removal (N = 18); also removed were four stepfathers, four male friends, three mothers, one teacher (who was removed from the school), and, on one occasion, both parents. In just under one-fourth of the cases of both black and white abuse, DPS noted continued delivery of protective services. Very few cases were noted as closed after confirmation.

Sexual Abuse in the State

In the twenty-five sample counties, 211 cases of sexual abuse were confirmed (see Table 7–2). As was shown in Table 7–3, the highest rate of sexual abuse was in Cherokee County; four counties (Clay, Coosa, Cleburne, and Franklin) had no confirmed sexual abuse. Forty-nine of the cases involved black female victims, 12 cases involved black males, 114 cases involved white females, and 36 cases involved white males; 29 percent of the victims were black and 71 percent were white. As discussed in the preceding chapter, the twenty-eight children who were both physically and sexually abused have been included in these numbers. The five black children (four girls) and six white children (all girls) who were raped were also included in the sexual abuse reports for analysis.

THE VICTIMS

In the vast majority (91 percent of the black, 85 percent of the white) of the reports, only one child was abused. In over two-thirds of the cases of white abuse and three-fourths of the cases of black abuse that involved a single victim, the child was the first-born or eldest child living in the house.

The sexual abuse rate for blacks was .32 and for whites, .42. Not surprisingly, girls were the victims of sexual abuse a great deal more frequently than boys. White girls in early adolescence (ten to fourteen years old) had the highest rate at 1.09; in all age

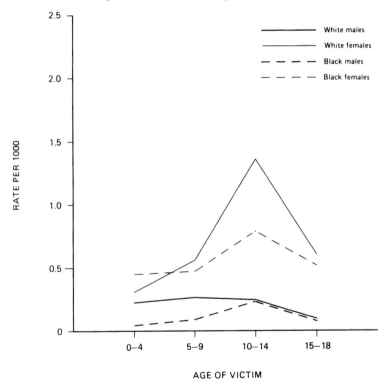

Figure 7-3   Rates of Sexual Abuse in Alabama

groups, with the exception of infancy, white girls had higher rates than black girls (see Figure 7–3). The proportion of sexually abused children who were female was slightly greater among blacks (80 percent) than whites (76 percent). In other words, slightly more white male children were the victims of sexual abuse than were black male children. Among boys, the rates were also higher for whites than for blacks, but the numbers were too small for both races to make reliable comparisons.

SMSA VERSUS NON-SMSA OR "URBAN" VERSUS "RURAL" ABUSE

Table 7–10 shows the statewide rates of sexual child abuse by the race and sex of the child as well as by the SMSA/non-SMSA designation. As explained previously, the SMSA, or standard metropolitan statistical area, is a statistical standard developed for use by the U.S. Office of Management and Budget. Each SMSA has one or more central counties containing the area's main population concentration. That county is usually referred to as having a metropolitan population, although it includes not only the urban population but also the population living in remote rural regions of the county. Nonetheless, the SMSA/non-SMSA rates of child abuse are reported here for comparison with other epidemiological studies.

Black boys had the lowest statewide sexual abuse rates. White children's rates of sexual abuse were virtually equivalent in both SMSA and non-SMSA areas. These rates represent the number of children abused divided by the appropriate population at risk (e.g., for white SMSA girls, the number of cases was divided by the total white female population below age eighteen in the sampled SMSA counties). The rates suggest that little association existed between the characteristics of metropolitan and non-metropolitan areas and the incidence of sexual abuse. Although the numbers are very small, it is interesting that black male sexual abuse required investigation almost as often in nonmetropolitan areas as it did in metropolitan areas, whereas 70 percent of the investigations of white boys took place in "urban" areas. Investigations of sexual abuse of black girls occurred more often in metropolitan areas (61 percent), but the rate of sexual abuse of black

Table 7-10

Rates of Sexual Abuse in SMSA/Non-SMSA by Race, Sex, and Age
of Victim

Victim	Age	SMSA	Non-SMSA
Black male		.09	.11
	0 - 4	.06	.00
	5 - 9	.06	.17
	10 - 14	.20	.14
	15 - 18	.06	.15
Black female		.43	.67
	0 - 4	.42	.24
	5 - 9	.52	.31
	10 - 14	.51	1.27
	15 - 18	.29	.95
White male		.19	.15
	0 - 4	.14	.22
	5 - 9	.28	.20
	10 - 14	.27	.07
	15 - 18	.08	.12
White female		.62	.58
	0 - 4	.26	.17
	5 - 9	.44	.51
	10 - 14	1.29	.70
	15 - 18	.47	.88

girls was actually highest in nonmetropolitan areas among children ten to fourteen years old. In fact, that rate (1.27) was virtually identical to the rate among metropolitan white girls of the same age (1.29).

THE CONTEXT OF ABUSE

The modal household in cases of black sexual abuse was made up of five people, including one (23 percent) or two (25 percent) children (the range of children was one to eight). In white sexual abuse, the modal household was smaller; it had only four members and, on the average, included two children (the range of children was one to ten).

As discussed earlier, the perpetrators of abuse and the types of households in which abuse occurred are highly interrelated. It is necessary, therefore, to take into account the proportions of various types of households among blacks and whites within the state as a whole in order to interpret the risks associated with household type and with the perpetrators of abuse. This step is equivalent to calculating rates by controlling for the size of the population at risk. In this case, one is controlling for the frequency of occurrence of household types in the population at large.

In our sample of confirmed cases of child abuse, as shown in Table 7–11, 37 percent of the black children lived in homes in which a female was designated the head of household. In Alabama, 35 percent of all black children live in these households, virtually a 1:1 ratio. One-third of all abused black girls and two-thirds of the abused black boys were from these households. Girls were also abused in stepfamilies almost as often as in homes with both of their biological parents (26 and 28 percent, respectively).

The abuse of white children reflected a different household pattern. White children lived in female-headed households in 23 percent of the sexual abuse cases; when compared to the 10 percent of the white population living in these households, there is a risk factor of 2.4, which is greater than that for black children. The highest frequency of sexual abuse of white girls, however, took place in stepfamilies (36 percent) and when the girl lived with both parents (31 percent).

When the children lived in a household headed by a woman, in both black and white abuse, the most frequent offender was a male friend of the mother. This trend was especially true in white households, where male friends were responsible for 32 percent of the sexual abuse. In black female-headed households, 22 percent

Table 7-11

Statewide Percentages of Sexual Abuse by Type of Household, Race,[*] and Sex of Victim

Household Type	Black			White		
	Male (N=8) vs.	Female (N=46)	% Total Abuse	Male (N=32) vs.	Female (N=103)	% Total Abuse
Female-headed	25.0	75.0	37.0	32.2	67.8	23.0
Both biological parents	—	100.0	24.1	30.4	69.6	34.1
Father only	—	—	—	30.0	70.0	7.4
Stepfamily	7.7	92.3	24.1	11.9	88.1	30.4
Other[**]	25.0	75.0	14.8	33.3	66.7	5.1

[*] $X^2=15.48$; df=7; p=.03

[**] refers to households in which a grandparent, a sibling, or an unknown person is the household head

of the abuse was perpetrated by a male friend. The women heading these households were divorced in two-thirds of white abuse; among blacks, they were divorced (24 percent), never married (28 percent), or their marital status was unknown (28 percent). Interestingly, none of the white women were in the category of "never been married."

As can be seen in Table 7–12, black parents abused only their daughters, not their sons. Overall, black girls were sexually abused in more than half the cases by a caretaker (an adult with whom the child lives) and in another fourth of the cases by someone unrelated to the victim; black boys, on the other hand, were sexually abused by a relative other than their caretaker in one-third of the cases and by an unrelated person in 56 percent of the cases. Obviously, caretakers accounted only for the remaining insignificant number of cases. White girls and boys were victims of

Table 7-12

Statewide Percentages of Perpetrators of Sexual Abuse by Race and
Sex of Victim

Perpetrator	Black			White		
	Male (N=9) vs.	Female (N=45)	% Total Abuse	Male (N=32) vs.	Female (N=104)	% Total Abuse
Father	—	100.0	14.8	21.6	78.4	27.2
Mother	—	100.0	1.9	50.0	50.0	1.5
Both biological parents	—	100.0	3.7	30.0	70.0	7.4
Stepfather	9.1	90.9	20.4	4.2	95.8	17.6
Uncle	40.0	60.0	9.3	—	100.0	8.8
Brother	—	100.0	5.6	—	100.0	3.7
Male friend	25.0	75.0	14.8	40.0	60.0	11.0
Neighbor	25.0	75.0	7.4	25.0	75.0	2.9
Anonymous	—	100.0	5.6	—	100.0	.7
Other*	38.0	62.0	16.5	24.0	76.0	19.6

*includes grandfather, foster and stepsiblings, brother-in-law, cousin, and a stranger

sexual abuse by a caretaker in more than 60 percent of the cases.
Other relatives and nonrelatives each accounted for approximately 20 percent of the sexual abuse of girls; white boys were
abused by unrelated persons in more than one-third of the cases.
In spite of the high prevalence of noncaretaker abuse, almost
three-fourths of all abuse occurred in the child's own home.

Abuse of boys by males (male homosexual abuse) was somewhat more prevalent among whites than blacks. In all, at least 13

percent of white sexual abuse and 11 percent of black sexual abuse was perpetrated by males on boys. These percentages may underestimate the actual figures inasmuch as several categories, such as neighbor, cousin, and so forth, did not identify the sex of the perpetrator. Only three instances were reported of sexual abuse by female perpetrators on girls; two cases were white, one black.

Among both black and white girls, 33 percent of sexual abuse was incestuous (defined here as abuse by a blood relative), and white fathers perpetrated sexual abuse against their daughters twice as often as black fathers. All other categories of perpetrators were roughly and equivalently distributed by race, with the exception of stepfathers and male friends of the child's mother, as previously discussed.

THE INJURIES RESULTING FROM SEXUAL ABUSE

A remarkable number of sexually abused children were acknowledged to have experienced psychological damage, as can be seen in Table 7–13. No explanation is given, however, as to why girls were four times more frequently mentioned as having suffered this type of damage. Many of the children also received bruises and cuts as a result of sexual abuse; both black and white boys were injured more often than girls. Three black girls contracted venereal disease, and eight pregnancies resulted from the sexual abuse, four within each race.

DISPOSITION OF CASES

Almost one-third of both the black and the white sexually abused children were removed, at least temporarily, from the home following investigation; 59 percent of the white children were placed with relatives, and an equivalent proportion of black children were placed in foster homes. Also equivalent for blacks and whites was the 23 percent of cases involving removal of the perpetrator from the home; among whites, fathers accounted for one-third of the total of white perpetrators removed.

Eleven black perpetrators (five male friends, two stepfathers, two neighbors, one father, and one uncle), were criminally

Table 7-13

Statewide Percentages of Children Receiving Injury in Sexual Abuse
by Type of Injury, Race, and Sex of Victim

	Black (N=55)			White (N=136)		
Injury	Male (N=9) vs.	Female (N=46)	% Total Abuse*	Male (N=32) vs.	Female (N=104)	% Total Abuse*
No injury	18.2	81.8	40.0	20.5	79.5	32.4
Bruises	—	100.0	9.1	39.1	60.9	16.9
Cuts	—	100.0	12.7	46.2	53.8	9.6
Fractures	—	—	—	50.0	50.0	1.5
Psychological effects	17.9	82.1	50.9	23.7	76.2	58.8

*Because some children received multiple injuries, the columns add
to more than 100 percent.

charged. Among the cases of white sexual abuse, forty perpetrators (eighteen fathers, six stepfathers, six male friends, two
grandfathers, two uncles, one each of a female friend, a brother, a
neighbor, a stranger, and two persons who were unidentified) were
criminally charged (27 percent of white sexual abuse). One-fourth
of the white children and half of the black children were medically
examined.

Summary

   These statewide findings may be helpful for an overall understanding of the problem of child abuse in Alabama; for elucidation
of factors that may contribute to abuse etiology, however, the analyses to follow will be more useful. The next chapters will present
the Alabama data within each of the three geographical units hypothesized to contribute to unique patterns of abuse characteristics.

8
The Ecological Context
of Physical Abuse

Unlike states outside the South, the history of the state of Alabama has been largely defined by two major ethnic or racial groups, black and white. They share a cultural experience, but, at the same time, each group has developed important and distinct cultural differences. These broad cultural traditions, which include attitudes toward marriage and child rearing, are modified by the social and economic realities of daily experience within one's smaller community. This investigation into the incidence of physical abuse supports the influence of these cultural and community differences.

As shown in Table 8–1, the ratio of Alabama's child population to the proportion of total abuse resulted in an overwhelming risk for both black and white children in communities outside of urbanized areas, but not in rural areas. The ratios of physical abuse in Alabama were somewhat greater for black than for white children, but, in terms of actual numbers, more white children than black were reported to the system. In other words, more investigations were conducted of white families than of black families, except in urbanized areas. Black girls were at considerably greater risk in larger communities, black boys in the smaller communities; nonetheless, white boys who live in towns and small cities were the children at greatest risk in Alabama. Detailed analysis of these and other characteristics of abuse in rural, midsized, and urban communities will be described in this chapter, followed by a summary.

Table 8-1

Comparison of Percentages of Physical Abuse to Percentages of Alabama Population Under 18 Living in Rural Areas, Outside Urbanized Areas, and Within Urbanized Areas in Alabama

Community Size	Black				White			
	N	% Black Abuse	% Black Population	Ratio	N	% White Abuse	% White Population	Ratio
Rural (<10,000)	57	24.5	41.2	.59	181	47.8	56.0	.85
Outside urbanized areas (10,000 – 50,000)	39	16.7	6.1	2.74	70	18.5	5.5	3.35
Urbanized areas (>50,000)	130	55.8	52.5	1.06	103	27.2	38.5	.70
Total	226	97.0			354	93.5		
Missing data	7	3.0			25	6.5		
Alabama total	233	100.0			379	100.0		

Physical Abuse in Rural Alabama

Although the rural areas of Alabama (including towns of fewer than 10,000 inhabitants) account for 49 percent of the state's population, only 39 percent (N = 238) of the reports of physical abuse came from these areas. (It cannot, however, be determined whether less abuse actually occurred in these areas or whether it simply was not reported as frequently.)

Of those residents under eighteen years of age, 56 percent of the whites and 41 percent of the blacks live in rural areas. The reports of abuse in rural areas made up 52 percent of the statewide white abuse but only 26 percent of the statewide black abuse. Reports of physical abuse from rural areas involved 57 black children and 181 white children (see Table 8–2).

Table 8–2

Physical Abuse in Rural Areas by Race and Sex of Victim

Sex	Black		White		Total	
	N	% of Abuse	N	% of Abuse	N	% of Abuse
Male	34	14.3	97	40.8	131	55.0
Female	23	9.7	84	35.3	107	45.0
Total	57	23.9	181	76.1	238	100.0

THE VICTIMS

Based on the founded reports, physical abuse in rural areas was slightly more prevalent among boys (55 percent) than girls; white children constituted 76 percent of the victims. The percentages of victims who were under the age of five were relatively equal when comparing both race and sex of the victims, although slightly more black females and white males were abused (see Figure 8–1). The percentages in the three age categories of children under age fifteen were equal (29 percent each) for white boys, but 41 percent of abused black boys were between five and nine years old. Both black and white boys aged fifteen and older were the least frequently abused. Physical abuse of both black

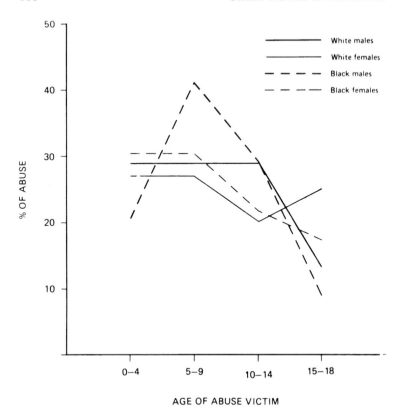

Figure 8–1   Frequency of Reports of Physical Abuse in Rural Areas by
             Sex, Race, and Age of Victim

and white girls occurred equally as often among infants and children aged five to nine. Among black girls, the figures continued to decline with age, but among white girls a greater frequency of abuse occurred after age fifteen than between the ages of ten and fourteen.

THE CONTEXT OF ABUSE

Ninety-six percent of abused black children and 81 percent of abused white children were victimized in their own homes. In 80 percent of the white families, one child was victimized, and in 12 percent, two children were victims. Among black families only one child was abused in 71 percent of the reports and two children in 17 percent; the range was one to five.

In 31 percent of the white cases and 24 percent of the black cases the victim was the only child in the family. There were two children in the home in two-thirds of the white families, with a range of one to four. The modal black family had four children, with a range of one to six. For those cases in which the birth order was known, 70 percent of the cases for both races involved the eldest child.

More than half of the physical abuse of blacks occurred to children in families headed by women, while less than a fifth of white abuse was directed against children who lived in female-headed households, as shown in Table 8–3. However, these apparent dif-

Table 8–3

Percentages of Physical Abuse in Rural Areas by Type of Household, Race, * and Sex of Victim

Household Type	Black			White		
	Male (N=31) vs.	Female (N=23)	% Total Abuse	Male (N=97) vs.	Female (N=83)	% Total Abuse
Female–headed	57.1	42.9	51.9	42.7	57.1	19.4
Both biological parents	71.4	28.6	25.9	52.6	47.4	43.3
Father only	—	100.0	1.9	22.2	77.8	5.0
Stepfamily	20.0	80.0	9.3	69.2	30.8	28.9
Other **	66.7	33.3	11.1	50.0	50.0	3.3

* $X^2=3.67$; df=4; NS

** refers to households in which a grandparent, sibling, or foster parent is the household head

ferences are reduced when one realizes that 32 percent of rural black families in the state were headed by females, compared to only 8 percent of the rural white families. These figures translate into a ratio of 3.2 for black physical abuse and of 5.2 for white physical abuse in female-headed households, indicating that white children who lived in these homes were at greater risk than were black children. The women heading their own households in this study were divorced and separated in one-fourth each of the black reports; almost half of these women had never been married. Half of the white women were divorced, one-fourth were separated, and only 11 percent were never married. It is clear that the set of circumstances that resulted in their heading their own households was markedly different for black and white women, and the household-type category obviously masks an underlying diversity.

Black boys were abused much more often than girls in families headed by a woman (57 to 43 percent) and in families with both biological parents present (71 percent of the incidents in those families). Black girls were physically abused more often in step-families.

White abuse shows distinctly different patterns from black abuse; 42 percent of the abuse of white males and 45 percent of that of white females occurred in families with both natural parents, where boys were abused only slightly more often. An additional 29 percent of the abuse of white children occurred in stepfamilies, where boys were abused more than 2:1 over girls. In female-headed households, daughters were abused 57 percent of the time.

Among white families, mothers were the perpetrators of abuse almost as frequently as were fathers (see Table 8–4), but 42 percent of physical abuse against black children was perpetrated by their mothers and only 23 percent by their fathers. However, as previously discussed, the distribution of female-headed households in rural areas differs between the races, so the presence of a father, abusive or not, presumably also differs. Overall, 91 percent of the physical abuse of white children and 75 percent of the abuse of black children in rural areas was committed by a caretaker (an adult with whom the child lives). In both races, boys were victims in slightly over half of these cases.

Table 8-4

Percentages of Perpetrators of Physical Abuse in Rural Areas
by Race and Sex of Victim

	Black			White		
Perpetrator	Male (N=34) vs.	Female (N=23)	% Total Abuse	Male (N=97) vs.	Female (N=84)	% Total Abuse
Father	69.2	30.8	22.8	50.0	50.0	30.9
Mother	50.0	50.0	42.1	52.9	47.1	28.2
Both biological parents	33.3	66.7	5.3	50.0	50.0	15.5
Stepfather	33.3	66.7	5.3	70.8	29.2	13.3
Stepmother	—	—	—	33.3	66.7	1.7
Grandfather	—	—	—	66.7	33.3	1.7
Grandmother	66.7	33.3	5.3	—	—	—
Uncle	100.0	—	1.8	—	100.0	.6
Aunt	100.0	—	3.5	—	100.0	.6
Sibling	100.0	—	1.8	—	—	—
Male friend	50.0	50.0	3.5	57.1	42.9	3.9
Other*	80.0	20.0	8.8	57.1	42.9	3.9

*
includes foster mother, adoptive father, teacher, neighbor, and
unidentified perpetrator

When a black father was the perpetrator of physical abuse,
however, 69 percent of the victims were boys. Black mothers
abused their sons and daughters in equal proportions but were
responsible for 52 percent of the total physical abuse of black girls
and only 35 percent of that of black boys. On the other hand,
abuse of white boys and girls occurred in equal proportions when

perpetrated by fathers alone or by both parents, and it was relatively equally distributed (53 percent for boys, 47 percent for girls)
when the mother was the abuser. White stepfathers, however,
abused stepsons over stepdaughters by a ratio of 7:3.

Noncaretaker abuse of black children was committed equally
by the victim's relatives and by nonrelatives, but black boys were
the victims 86 percent of the time when the perpetrator was another relative and 71 percent of the time when the abuse was committed by a nonrelative.

THE INJURIES RESULTING FROM ABUSE

Most of the physically abused children from rural areas showed
some sign of the abuse; only 18 percent of the black children and

Table 8–5

Percentages of Children in Rural Areas Receiving Injury in
Physical Abuse by Type of Injury, Race, and Sex of Victim

Injury	Black			White		
	Male (N=34) vs.	Female (N=23)	% Total Abuse*	Male (N=97) vs.	Female (N=84)	% Total Abuse*
No injury	90.0	10.0	17.8	52.2	47.8	12.7
Bruises	54.5	45.5	77.2	54.5	45.5	72.9
Burns	—	—	—	—	100.0	1.1
Cuts	45.5	54.5	19.3	68.8	31.3	8.8
Fractures	—	100.0	1.8	62.5	37.5	4.4
Neurological	—	—	—	—	100.0	1.1
Psychological effects	33.3	66.7	15.8	65.9	34.1	24.3

*Because some children received multiple injuries, columns add to
more than 100 percent.

13 percent of the white children were not injured. Of children of both races, black girls were the most likely to be injured and black boys the least likely. Only 4 percent of the black girls, compared with 27 percent of the black boys, were uninjured. Preschool black boys received the greatest proportion of injuries; black girls, especially the younger ones, received multiple injuries. Relatively equal percentages of white boys and girls did not exhibit any signs of injury, and injuries were equivalent across all age levels.

Bruises were the most common injury among boys and girls of both races, but cuts were twice as common among blacks as among whites (see Table 8–5). Psychological injuries were received by more than one-fourth of the black girls and fewer than 10 percent of the boys; only one of the black children had any other type of injury. Psychological injuries were inflicted on 30 percent of the white boys and 18 percent of the white girls.

All physically abused rural black children reported by relatives had some visible injury; 65 percent were bruised and 35 percent were cut. When white relatives reported abuse, injuries were found in 90 percent of the cases. Injuries were reported in 80 percent of the black cases and 64 percent of the white cases when the reporter was a professional. Of the cases reported by other sources, such as friends and neighbors, injuries were reported in 71 percent of the black cases and 77 percent of the white cases.

DISPOSITION OF CASES

Physically abused white children from rural areas were removed from their homes more often than were black children (22 percent for whites, 16 percent for blacks). Three black infants were removed: one to a relative, one to foster care, and another to an unidentified location. Of those removed, about half the white children, especially the older ones, went to homes of relatives, and fourteen were placed in foster care (three infants, one preschooler, seven preadolescents, and three teenagers). Six other white children were removed, but their placement was not mentioned.

The perpetrator of abuse was removed from the household in only two cases of black abuse (in both instances it was the child's father) but in fifteen cases of white abuse: five fathers, three mothers, three stepfathers, two male friends of the mother; in one instance, both parents were removed and, in another, an unknown perpetrator.

Physical Abuse in Towns and Small Cities

Twenty black males, nineteen black females, forty-four white males, and twenty-six white females were victims of physical abuse in our sample of Alabama's towns and small cities (see Table 8–6).

Table 8–6

Physical Abuse in Towns and Small Cities by Race and Sex of Victim

	Black		White		Total	
Sex	N	% of Abuse	N	% of Abuse	N	% of Abuse
Male	20	18.3	44	40.4	64	58.7
Female	19	17.4	26	23.9	45	41.3
Total	39	35.7	70	64.3	109	100.0

The Victims

Sixty-seven percent of all confirmed abuse in these midsized communities was physical; almost two-thirds of physical abuse was of white children, with boys victimized almost twice as often as girls. In fact, 40 percent of all physical abuse in towns and small cities was abuse of white boys. Equivalent proportions of black boys and girls were victims.

Four-fifths of abuse of both black and white children involved one victim. The range was one to five among black families and one to three among white families. As shown in Figure 8–2, the frequency curve of abuse and age of the victim peaked for black girls in infancy, for black boys in the group aged five to nine. Among whites, the relationship by sex and age was very different. White male abuse was inversely related to age: it started very high in infancy (34 percent) and in preschool years (28 percent) and then steadily declined to a low of 15 percent in adolescence. Among white girls, however, only 16 percent of their total abuse was during infancy and 35 percent during the age range of five to nine years; during adolescence, the girls experienced 27 percent of their total abuse. In the adolescent age group (fifteen to eighteen), a major difference between the races emerged: only 9 percent of all black abuse involved adolescent victims compared to 18 percent of all white abuse.

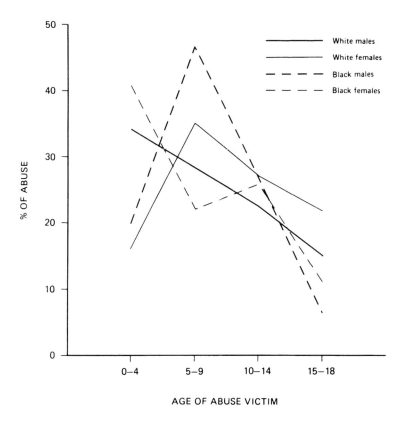

Figure 8–2   Frequency of Reports of Physical Abuse in Towns and Small Cities by Sex, Race, and Age of Victim

THE CONTEXT OF ABUSE

All but two incidents of white abuse occurred in the child's
home; six cases of black abuse occurred elsewhere, such as at the
homes of neighbors or relatives or in public places. The modal (31
percent) black household had four members, three of whom were
children; the number of children ranged from one to five. White
households also had four members, with one adult as often as two
(42 percent each) and, although the mode and mean were each
two children, 20 percent of the households had one child and 20
percent had three children. The range was from one to five.

Two-thirds of black abuse, but less than one-fifth of white physical abuse, occurred in female-headed households, as shown in
Table 8–7. Not surprisingly, these proportions were generally related to the proportions of living arrangements for all children in
midsized communities. However, the proportion of black children

Table 8–7

Percentages of Physical Abuse in Towns and Small Cities by
Type of Household, Race,* and Sex of Victim

Household Type	Black			White		
	Male (N=20) vs.	Female (N=19)	% Total Abuse	Male (N=44) vs.	Female (N=26)	% Total Abuse
Female–headed	50.0	50.0	66.7	46.5	53.5	18.6
Both biological parents	57.1	42.9	17.9	68.0	32.0	35.7
Father only	—	—	—	66.7	33.3	4.3
Stepfamily	40.0	60.0	12.8	65.5	34.5	41.4
Other**	100.0	—	2.6	—	—	—

* X^2=28.92; df=4; p=.00

** refers to a grandparent's household

who lived in households headed by women in these communities was 41 percent; therefore, a child faced a risk ratio of 1.62 if he or she lived in a household headed by a woman. Among white children living in these households, the proportion of children abused (19 percent) and in the population at large (12 percent) yields a ratio of 1.52. Therefore, both races were clearly at some risk in female-headed households. The greatest prevalence of abuse of white children, however, was when they lived with their biological parents (36 percent of all white abuse) or stepparents (41 percent). The ratio of white to black abuse in stepfamilies, however, was over 3:1.

In both black and white abuse, the proportion of male victims to female victims of physical abuse in female-headed households was roughly equivalent (1:1). The mother was the perpetrator of abuse in well over four-fifths (89 percent) of these black cases and in two-thirds (69 percent) of the white cases. When black children were living with both biological parents, boys were victims 57 percent of the time; among white families, boys were abused in 68 percent of the cases. In addition, white boys were abused over girls 2:1 in stepfamilies.

Caretakers of the children represented the overwhelming majority of all abuse: 91 percent of all physical abuse in towns and small cities was by a caretaker (an adult with whom the child lived) of a white child, with boys outnumbering girls 2:1; 87 percent of all black abuse was by a caretaker, with boys being abused only slightly more than girls. An overwhelming 69 percent of all black physical abuse was by the child's mother, as shown in Table 8–8. Ranked second was the child's father at a distant 8 percent. The remaining abuse was divided among stepparent(s), grandparent(s), other relative(s), and so forth. White boys were physically abused most often by their biological and stepfathers. White mothers were the perpetrators of physical abuse in 24 percent of the total.

THE INJURIES RESULTING FROM ABUSE

In almost three-fourths of the cases of black and white children, bruises resulted from their physical abuse (see Table 8–9). White

Table 8–8

Percentages of Perpetrators of Physical Abuse in Towns and Small
Cities by Race and Sex of Victim

Perpetrator	Black			White		
	Male (N=20) vs.	Female (N=19)	% Total Abuse	Male (N=44) vs.	Female (N=26)	% Total Abuse
Father	66.7	33.3	7.7	64.0	36.0	35.7
Mother	59.2	40.8	69.2	52.9	47.1	24.3
Both biological parents	—	100.0	2.6	100.0	—	1.4
Stepfather	100.0	—	2.6	69.2	30.8	18.6
Stepmother	—	100.0	5.1	71.4	28.6	10.0
Male friend	—	—	—	50.0	50.0	2.9
Other*	20.0	80.0	12.8	60.0	40.0	7.1

*includes foster mother, adoptive father, adoptive mother,
grandparent, female babysitter, teacher, and neighbor

children (70 percent of them boys) suffered fractured bones 10:1 over black children. Cuts were also reported in roughly 28 percent of all children. Interestingly, psychological damage to the child was mentioned in the reports for black children in 23 percent of the cases but in only 13 percent of the white cases (including only two white girls). One black infant girl died as a result of the physical injuries. One white child suffered neurological damage, and one suffered from burns; no black children had equivalent injuries.

DISPOSITION OF CASES

Children of either race were rarely removed from the household following abuse confirmation: five white infants and three teenagers were removed to relatives' homes, and three school-age

Table 8-9

Percentages of Children in Towns and Small Cities Receiving Injury
in Physical Abuse by Type of Injury, Race, and Sex of Victim

Injury	Black			White		
	Male (N=20) vs.	Female (N=19)	% Total Abuse	Male (N=44) vs.	Female (N=26)	% Total Abuse
No injury	55.5	44.5	23.0	88.8	11.2	12.8
Bruises	53.5	46.5	71.7	57.4	42.6	77.1
Burns	—	—	—	100.0	—	1.4
Cuts	46.1	53.9	33.3	66.7	33.3	25.7
Death	—	100.0	2.5	—	—	—
Fractures	—	100.0	2.5	70.0	30.0	14.3
Neurological	—	—	—	—	100.0	1.4
Psychological effects	33.3	66.7	23.1	77.7	22.3	12.9

*
Because some children received multiple injuries, columns add to
more than 100 percent

children were placed in foster care. Three black teenagers went to
relatives' homes, and five children were placed in foster homes.
The perpetrator was removed in six white cases (five fathers and
one stepfather) and one black case (a stepfather).

The perpetrator was criminally charged in only four cases of
physical abuse to black children and in five cases of abuse to
white children. Black mothers were arrested in three cases and an
aunt in one. Four white fathers and one brother were criminally
charged.

Physical Abuse in Urbanized Areas

Fifty-five percent of Alabama's black population and 42 percent
of Alabama's white population under eighteen years of age live in

urbanized areas. Obviously, by definition, urban areas have a dense population concentration and all the associated positive and negative features. Investigating abuse in urban areas introduces hardships unlike those found in smaller communities. While the number of actual resources available to assist in cases of abuse may be larger in urban areas, the complexity and bureaucracy of these resources can contribute to frustrations and delay.

In urbanized areas, fifty-eight black males, seventy-two black females, fifty-seven white males, and forty-six white females were victims of physical abuse (see Table 8–10).

THE VICTIMS

Black female children were the target of almost one-third of all abuse in urban areas; black and white male children were each abused in 25 percent of the reports, and white females had the lowest incidence at 20 percent of the total (see Table 8–10).

Among the black girls, the incidence of abuse was lowest in infancy and peaked in early adolescence; for boys, it peaked in the age group five to nine years old, then fell very low in the later adolescent period. Among white children, the incidence of abuse was somewhat more uniform across all ages (see Figure 8–3). The elevated frequency of black boys in the age group five to nine years old may be explained by the greater number of school system referrals of black children in general; one would expect a rise

Table 8–10

Physical Abuse in Urbanized Areas by Race and Sex of Victim

	Black		White		Total	
Sex	N	% of Abuse	N	% of Abuse	N	% of Abuse
Male	58	24.9	57	24.5	115	49.4
Female	72	30.9	46	19.7	118	50.6
Total	130	55.8	103	44.2	233	100.0

in the incidence of reports as children enter school and then later a decrease as they drop out from that surveillance system. Abuse of black girls, however, remains high throughout their teens, but the reason why the schools failed to report white children cannot be explained.

THE CONTEXT OF ABUSE

Almost all abuse occurred in the child's home. Most of the remaining 12 percent was abuse that occurred more than once and

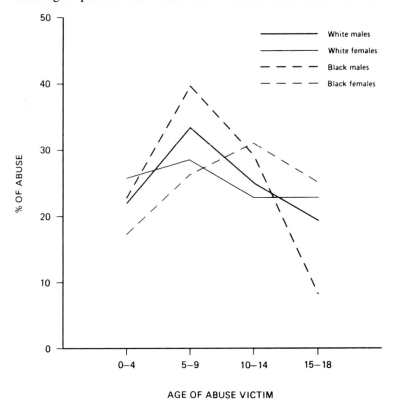

Figure 8–3 Frequency of Reports of Physical Abuse in Urbanized Areas by Sex, Race, and Age of Victim

in a variety of places. Although there was slightly more abuse in families with two children, both black and white physical abuse took place in roughly equal proportions of one-, two-, and three-child families. The range within black families (one to nine) was slightly larger than in white families (one to six). Thirty-two percent of the black households had one adult, and 45 percent had two adults, with a range from one to nine. Almost two-thirds of the white households had two adult members, with a range of one to six. Most abuse involved one victim (83 percent of black, 80 percent of white); the range was one to five among black families, one to three in white families.

As shown in Table 8–11, more than half of black physical abuse in urbanized areas took place in female-headed households. Inasmuch as 37 percent of all households in urban areas were headed by women, the result is a risk ratio of 1.4 for black chil-

Table 8–11

Percentages of Physical Abuse in Urbanized Areas by Type of Household, Race,* and Sex of Victim

Household Type	Black			White		
	Male (N=58) vs.	Female (N=72)	% Total Abuse	Male (N=57) vs.	Female (N=46)	% Total Abuse
Female-headed	39.0	61.0	53.1	52.3	47.7	20.4
Both biological parents	34.7	65.3	17.7	52.2	47.8	42.7
Father only	100.0	—	1.5	75.0	25.0	3.9
Stepfamily	60.8	39.2	17.7	63.3	36.7	29.1
Other**	53.8	46.2	10.0	25.0	75.0	3.9

* $X^2=35.89$; df=4; p=.00
** refers to households in which a foster parent, a grandparent, a sibling, or an unknown person is the household head

dren compared to a 2.3 for white children living in similar households.

Children with their biological parents and those living with stepparents accounted for equivalent proportions (18 percent each) of black abuse. The picture was quite different for white children; 43 percent of white abuse occurred in families with both biological parents, and stepfamilies accounted for 29 percent. In all, 86 percent of black children and 84 percent of white children were abused while living with a caretaker.

Within households headed by women, as well as in those with both biological parents, black girls were abused at least 3:2 over boys. However, in stepfamilies black boys were at greater risk (61 percent). Nonetheless, female-headed households were a greater risk to blacks of both sexes than any other household type.

In white abuse, on the other hand, the sexes were abused approximately equivalently in female-headed households and in households with both biological parents. However, in both stepfamilies and father-only families, white boys and black boys were abused more than girls.

As shown in Table 8–12, in urbanized areas black fathers and stepfathers were more likely to abuse their daughters (55 percent each). Black mothers, as well as both parents together, also appeared to victimize their daughters; all in all, black girls were targeted with a much greater frequency than were black boys. Over half of all black abuse was perpetrated by the child's mother. In white families, mothers perpetrated the abuse in just slightly more than a fourth of the cases.

It seems clear that divergent cultural factors were at work when these black relationships are compared to white relationships. White fathers, for example, abused their sons in over two-thirds of the reports of father-perpetrated abuse; stepfathers abused stepsons more than twice as often as they abused their stepdaughters. White women (mothers, stepmothers, and grandmothers) and their male friends abused girls more frequently than boys. Both parents, when they abused together, abused their daughters in every instance. In white families, there was a marked tendency for a parent to abuse the same-sex child, whereas there was a greater tendency in black families to abuse the daughter, regardless of the sex of the perpetrator.

Table 8–12

Percentages of Perpetrators of Physical Abuse in Urbanized Areas
by Race and Sex of Victim

	Black			White		
Perpetrator	Male (N=58) vs.	Female (N=72)	% Total Abuse	Male (N=57) vs.	Female (N=46)	% Total Abuse
Father	45.0	55.0	15.4	70.0	30.0	36.3
Mother	41.7	58.3	51.5	46.4	53.6	27.2
Both biological parents	28.5	71.5	5.4	—	100.0	5.8
Stepfather	45.5	54.5	8.5	72.7	27.3	9.8
Stepmother	33.3	66.7	2.3	33.3	66.7	2.9
Grandmother	80.0	20.0	3.8	33.3	66.7	2.9
Uncle	50.0	50.0	1.5	—	—	—
Aunt	50.0	50.0	1.5	—	—	—
Brother	—	100.0	.8	—	100.0	1.9
Male friend	40.0	60.0	3.8	44.4	55.6	8.7
Other*	60.0	40.0	4.5	—	100.0	4.0

*
includes foster and adoptive mothers, brother-in-law, female
babysitter, and teacher

THE INJURIES RESULTING FROM ABUSE

Table 8–13 shows the injuries sustained by the abused children
in urbanized areas. Most frequent were bruises and cuts, especially among black children. Only black children sustained
fractures. One black infant died of the injuries inflicted, but no
details of this case were included in the narrative report. One out

Table 8–13

Percentages of Children in Urbanized Areas Receiving Injury in
Physical Abuse by Type of Injury, Race, and Sex of Victim

	Black			White		
Injury	Male (N=58) $^{vs.}$	Female (N=72)	% Total Abuse	Male (N=57) $^{vs.}$	Female (N=46)	% Total Abuse
No injury	50.0	50.0	7.8	54.5	45.4	10.6
Bruises	45.6	54.4	79.2	54.7	45.3	81.5
Burns	62.5	37.5	6.2	100.0	—	.9
Cuts	45.2	54.8	23.8	53.8	46.2	12.6
Deaths	—	100.0	.7	—	—	—
Fractures	54.5	45.5	9.8	—	—	—
Neurological	50.0	50.0	3.0	100.0	—	.9
Psychological effects	16.6	83.4	9.2	50.0	50.0	13.5

*
 Because some children received multiple injuries, columns add
to more than 100 percent

of four children, both black and white, was evaluated by a physician or by hospital personnel following his or her injuries. Psychological effects on the child were noted in fewer than 14 percent
of the cases; caseworkers reported these effects in black female
victims 5:1 over male victims, but among white children there
were no sex differences.

DISPOSITION OF CASES

In a remarkable 41 percent of black abuse and 34 percent of
white abuse, the child was at least temporarily removed from the
household. Thirty percent of the black children who were re-

moved were placed with a relative, and 49 percent went into foster care. Forty-seven percent of the white children who were removed were placed with a relative, and an equal proportion were placed in a foster home.

In at least 8 percent of black abuse and 11 percent of white abuse incidents, the perpetrator was removed from the household. Among blacks, two fathers, two mothers, four stepfathers, an uncle, and in one case, both parents were removed; among whites, eight fathers, one grandmother, and two male friends were removed. Perpetrators were rarely charged criminally: three black and three white fathers, one black mother, both parents of a white child, one teacher of a black child, and two male friends of the mothers of white children.

Many of the narrative reports were limited in detail; any further analysis of the disposition of cases in urbanized areas, due to the large amount of missing information, would be unreliable.

Summary

Community size and the sex of the physically abused victim were clearly interrelated, although a relationship by race, sex, and community size was not statistically significant. For example, among black children in rural areas, boys were abused more often; in towns and small cities, abuse of black boys and girls was equal; but in urbanized areas, black girls were far more frequent targets. For white children, the pattern of community size and abuse was no less confounding. In rural areas, boys were abused slightly more often; in the midsized communities, boys were victimized almost twice as often as girls; and in urban areas, they were abused only slightly more frequently.

These patterns suggest that different cultural factors, both racial and demographic, contribute to the physical abuse of black and white children. If one accepts the theory, as indicated by the literature, that abuse is largely the result of stress and frustration displaced upon a child, in rural areas the black boy either represented the seed of the malcontent or a more "acceptable" (whether personally or culturally) target for aggression. This pattern was also true for white families in towns and small cities—

the boys were the overwhelming favorites for abuse. Perhaps the sex role ideology of these cultures identified as problematic the misbehavior of a male child and accepted the use of physical punishment for his "misdeeds." This hypothesis was supported in part by the larger percentage of all abuse cases in towns and small cities declared by the investigator to have resulted from the care-takers' excessive disciplinary style: 24 percent of white cases, compared to 16 percent in both rural and urban places. Among blacks, the relationship was a straight linear one, with 20 percent of the rural black families considered harsh disciplinarians, 16 percent in the midsized communities, and only 10 percent in the urban areas.

The age, sex, and race of children reported to the system were also interrelated. Within each community size, reports were made for infants, elementary-age children, preadolescents, and teen-agers. By comparing the proportions of children within each age group among community sizes, one can see which areas experi-enced increased vigilance or surveillance of each group. As was shown in Figures 8–1, 8–2, and 8–3, among black boys, the over-all age of reporting was curvilinear, peaking in the age group of five to nine years; the younger boys were reported from less densely populated areas, the midsized communities especially, and with a distinct decrease in reports as the child aged. Black girls were more evenly reported across community sizes in gen-eral, with the exception of a very high proportion of infant reports from towns and small cities. White boys, in contrast to black boys, had a regular pattern of reports by age and community size, with only a slight inverse relationship. It is interesting that white infant girls were rarely reported from the same midsized commu-nities that reported black infant girls in such great proportions. In addition, white girls were consistently reported within all commu-nities in spite of their increase in age.[1]

Families can be characterized, at least in part, by the source of power and authority within the household, a characterization that also provides clues to child abuse etiology. For example, in both rural and urban areas, about half of all black abuse took place in homes headed by a woman, but in towns and small cities, female-headed households were the context for two-thirds of abuse. The proportion of abuse in homes with both of the child's original parents decreased as the community size increased, while stepfamily abuse was positively related to community size.

Interestingly, black boys and girls in households in which the mother was the designated head, and by far the most frequent perpetrator, were abused in equal proportions in rural areas and midsized communities. In other words, these mothers were apparently indifferent to the gender of the child with respect to the form of their punishment or discipline. In urbanized areas, however, where white children in female-headed households were abused almost equally regardless of sex, black girls were victimized 3:2 over boys; both their mothers and their fathers abused them more often than they abused boys. The reverse was true both in towns and small cities and in rural areas, where boys were the favorite targets. City culture is apparently less protective of these young black girls than the more traditional nonurban cultures. There are many interesting—but hypothetical—explanations. For example, city life may provoke a girl to more acting-out behavior; black boys may be protected from abuse due to the assignment of adult status at an earlier age than in the country; the extended kin support network found in rural areas and midsized communities, but not in the larger cities, may especially protect the female children from abuse.

White abuse was remarkably similar in both rural and urban communities, with roughly 20 percent taking place in female-headed households and 40 percent in homes with both of the child's original parents. Interestingly, however, towns and small cities presented a different picture, for both whites and blacks. In these communities, the proportion of abuse taking place in white stepfamilies was higher than that either in female-headed families or in families with both original parents. Because stepfathers accounted for almost a fifth of the abuse and targeted their stepsons twice as often as their stepdaughters, their presence was a major factor in the very high rates of abuse of young white boys in these communities.

The findings of this study indicate that a combination of racial and cultural factors modify the targets of abuse. A clear pattern emerged of men being most aggressive toward young white boys, especially in the towns and small cities, and of women against young white girls. Within black families, the gender of abuser and the victim were unrelated outside of urbanized areas.

Distinct racial and community patterns also occurred in the types of injuries from which the abused children suffered. For example, although no injuries were reported in a fourth of black children in the midsized communities, those who were injured received multiple injuries, especially cuts, bruises, and psychological trauma. It is also in these same communities that the greatest proportion of white children received cuts and fractures. In other words, towns and small cities were communities in which the victims, white children especially, appeared to be suffering from the more serious forms of physical injury. Yet they were not reported to suffer emotionally as often as in communities in which their injuries had been less profound. Because psychological damage is almost assured in cases of child abuse, the notation of such injury may be more a reflection of caseworker sensitivity (or commitment to detail) than it is of actual injury to the child.

It is clear that the communities that present the greatest mystery are the midsized towns and small cities. The rates of abuse and the injuries incurred in these areas were far greater than those in either rural or urbanized communities. Before one can conclude that these communities represented the regions of greatest abuse, however, it is important to consider an alternate possibility—that these communities represented the reporting-surveillance system working at its best. The evidence is certainly equivocal. Although black and white children lived in equal proportions in these towns, whites were overrepresented among the abused; white children were also more seriously abused in these communities than elsewhere. Reports of abuse were received predominantly from institutions, but their reporting patterns were not significantly different from those in urbanized areas. Friends and neighbors of black children made no reports. Fathers and especially stepfathers accounted for more of the white abuse in these communities than elsewhere and, furthermore, were far more likely to abuse their sons than daughters. These details add up to a high-risk environment for young white boys who live with a father or father figure in towns and small cities, but they do not tell us whether the risk is of being abused or of being reported. If it is the latter, these communities can give us important clues to an effective system. On the other hand, if the former explanation is correct, these communities can provide a greater understanding of the factors that contribute to physical abuse. An answer to this dilemma is worth pursuing.

Note

1. The relationship between the age of the victim and the size of the community was statistically significant only for black children.

9
The Ecological Context
of Sexual Abuse

Half of the reported incidents of sexual abuse in Alabama were confirmed by the caseworker investigator, but the final number of sexual abuse incidents, especially when considered within their respective community types, was remarkably small. Nonetheless, as with physical abuse, the ratio of the frequency of sexual abuse to the proportion of Alabama population within these communities, as shown in Table 9–1, resulted in increased risk for both black and white children in midsized communities. Unlike physical abuse, however, few clear patterns emerged among reporters or perpetrators. This study would appear to support the existing literature, which finds that the incidence of sexual abuse is not greatly influenced by external environmental or community-related factors.

Sexual Abuse in Rural Areas

Although almost half (49 percent) of Alabama's population lived in rural areas (including towns with fewer than 10,000 inhabitants) in 1980, only 42 percent of the 191 reports of abuse that could be geographically identified in 1982 involved children from rural areas. Of these reports, 75 percent involved white victims and 25 percent involved black victims; these figures compared with a rural population under eighteen years of age that is 79 percent white and 20 percent black. The black victims included fourteen girls and six boys; the white victims included forty-seven girls and fourteen boys (see Table 9–2). Ten of the white children were both physically and sexually abused, as were two black children.

123

Table 9-1

Comparison of Percentages of Sexual Abuse to Percentages of Alabama Population Under 18 Living in Rural Areas, Outside Urbanized Areas, and Within Urbanized Areas

Community Size	Black				White			
	N	% Black Abuse	% Black Population	Ratio	N	% White Abuse	% White Population	Ratio
Rural (<10,000)	20	32.8	41.2	.78	61	40.7	56.0	.73
Outside urbanized areas (10,000 – 50,000)	12	19.7	6.1	3.23	32	21.3	5.5	3.87
Urbanized areas (>50,000)	22	36.1	52.5	.69	44	29.3	38.5	.76
Total	54	88.6			137	91.3		
Missing data	7	11.4			13	8.7		
Alabama total	61	100.0			150	100.0		

Table 9–2

Sexual Abuse in Rural Areas by Race and Sex of Victim

Sex	Black		White		Total	
	N	% of Abuse	N	% of Abuse	N	% of Abuse
Male	6	7.4	14	17.3	20	24.7
Female	14	17.3	47	58.0	61	75.3
Total	20	24.7	61	75.3	81	100.0

Many of the results that follow are reported in percentages; it is important to realize, however, that the actual number of reports within categories is often small. For example, each report of a sexually abused black boy represents 17 percent of those reports. Nonetheless, these data accurately reflect the confirmed sexual abuse that occurred in rural areas.

THE VICTIMS

As might be expected, girls were the victims of sexual abuse more often than boys, as is shown in Table 9–2; three-fourths of sexual abuse reports involved a female victim. This proportion was slightly lower among blacks than among whites. Black boys were the least frequently abused group, and white girls were the most frequently abused. It is interesting to note that the proportions of rural sexual abuse reports involving white boys and black girls were equal.

Children between the ages of ten and fourteen were the most frequent victims of sexual abuse. Children in that early adolescent range accounted for 45 percent of black abuse and 43 percent of white abuse, for 40 percent of abuse of boys and 44 percent of abuse of girls. The proportions of sexually abused white boys were equal (36 percent) for ages five to nine and ten to fourteen; half of the abused black boys were between ten and fourteen and another third were fifteen or older. Sexual abuse involving girls of both races peaked in the age group ten to fourteen years old (43 percent for blacks, 45 percent for whites). Girls aged fifteen and older were the next most frequently abused, with 36 percent of the black girls and 26 percent of the white girls falling into that age group.

The Context of Abuse

Most sexual abuse of rural children occurred in the victim's own home (75 and 72 percent for black and white children, respectively). White children were abused in a relative's house in 12 percent of the cases; no confirmed incidents of black abuse took place in a relative's house.

Approximately one-third of the reports of both races involved a victim who was the only child in the home (33 percent of blacks, 32 percent of whites). The percentages of victims from homes with two children were also relatively equal (27 percent for blacks, 29 percent for whites). When birth order was considered, however, the proportions changed. Three-quarters of the black victims were first-born children, but only 64 percent of the white victims were. Cases involving more than one victim in the home were also slightly more common among blacks (17 percent) than whites (11 percent).

As can be seen in Table 9–3, sexual abuse in both races occurred most often in two-parent families; 53 percent of black abuse and 61 percent of white abuse occurred to children living with two parents; 63 percent of rural black families and 89 percent of rural white families live in two-parent households. Although 32 percent of black sexual abuse in rural areas involved children in female-headed households, these families also constituted 32 percent of the population, so, unlike those in communities of other sizes, rural children were not at heightened risk in female-headed households. Women head only 8 percent of the white families in rural areas, yet a full quarter of sexual abuse was perpetrated against children in these households, a ratio of 3:1. White children in female-headed households, unlike black chidren, were therefore at great risk of sexual abuse.

Caretakers (adults with whom the child lived) were responsible for 62 percent of white sexual abuse; they committed 64 percent of

Table 9–3

Percentages of Sexual Abuse in Rural Areas by Type of Household and
Race of Victim

Household Type	Black (N=19)	White (N=60)
Female–headed	31.6	25.0
Both biological parents	26.3	36.7
Father only	—	8.3
Stepfamily	26.3	23.3
Unknown	15.8	6.7

the abuse against white boys and 62 percent of that against white girls. An additional 21 percent of abuse of white girls was committed by other relatives. White boys, however, were abused in over a third of the cases by nonrelatives, including friends, neighbors, babysitters, and strangers. Interestingly, when male friends sexually abused white children, the victim was a boy in 60 percent of the cases.

Black children, on the other hand, were sexually abused by caretakers in only 40 percent of the cases, and most of the children abused were girls. Other relatives accounted for 30 percent of black sexual abuse and other nonrelatives for 25 percent.

In rural areas, fathers and stepfathers accounted for 26 and 16 percent, respectively, of the sexual abuse of white children (see Table 9–4) and for 5 and 20 percent of sexual abuse of black children. A sizable frequency of sexual abuse of white children was included in the "other" category.

Several perpetrator categories (such as neighbor, cousin, etc.) do not identify the sex of the perpetrator, making homosexual abuse difficult to quantify. However, at least five out of the six cases (83 percent) of black male sexual abuse were definitely homosexual abuse, with stepfathers, grandfathers, uncles, and male friends the known perpetrators; 64 percent of abuse to white boys was homosexual. (Four fathers and three male friends were the

Table 9–4

Percentages of Perpetrators of Sexual Abuse in Rural Areas by
Race of Victim

Perpetrator	Black	White
Father	5.0 (N=1)	26.2 (N=16)
Mother	—	3.3 (N=2)
Both biological parents	5.0 (N=1)	8.2 (N=5)
Stepfather	20.0 (N=4)	16.4 (N=10)
Grandfather	10.0 (N=2)	1.6 (N=1)
Uncle	15.0 (N=3)	11.5 (N=7)
Brother	5.0 (N=1)	3.3 (N=2)
Male friend	15.0 (N=3)	8.2 (N=5)
Other *	20.0 (N=4)	14.7 (N=9)
Unknown	5.0 (N=1)	6.6 (N=4)

*
  includes adoptive father, brother-in-law, stepsibling, cousin,
  neighbor, and female friend

perpetrators.) No homosexual abuse of black girls was reported,
and only two cases of homosexual abuse of white girls occurred,
one by a mother and one by a female friend of the mother.

THE INJURIES RESULTING FROM ABUSE

Psychological injuries were reported in more than half of the
cases of sexual abuse. Among blacks, 64 percent of the girls and
50 percent of the boys were injured psychologically; most of these
girls (67 percent) were reported by an institution, and all reports
involved girls aged ten years and older. The percentages of cases

involving psychological injury were even higher for white children; 64 percent of the boys and 66 percent of the girls suffered psychological injury. These children were most often reported by a relative (67 percent of the boys, 55 percent of the girls). White girls were bruised in 17 percent of the reports, but other injuries were uncommon for both races. No injury at all was reported in 35 percent of the black cases and in 25 percent of the white cases. Forty percent of the sexually abused black children, compared with 26 percent of the white children, were examined by a physician. Two of the black boys and one white girl contracted venereal disease. Three white girls and three black girls became pregnant as a result of the abuse.

DISPOSITION OF CASES

The perpetrator of black abuse was removed from the home in 29 percent of the cases (one father, one uncle, and two male friends), all of which involved sexual abuse of girls. Those who abused white children (four fathers, three stepfathers, an uncle, a male friend, an adoptive father, and, in one instance, both parents) were removed in 21 percent of the cases. Arrests of the perpetrator occurred in three black cases (one father and two male friends) and in thirteen white cases (five fathers, three stepfathers, three male friends, a female friend, and a neighbor).

Twelve white children were removed from their homes, six to homes of relatives and six into foster care. Five black children were also relocated, one to a relative's house, three to foster homes, and one to an unidentified placement.

Sexual Abuse in Towns and Small Cities

As described in chapter 8, towns and small cities outside of urbanized areas represent unique sociological characteristics. Although approximately 6 percent of Alabama's population lives in these communities, at least 20 percent (N = 12) of all black and 21 percent (N = 32) of all white sexual abuse in Alabama took place in these midsized communities.

Table 9–5

Sexual Abuse in Towns and Small Cities by Race and Sex of Victim

Sex	Black		White		Total	
	N	% of Abuse	N	% of Abuse	N	% of Abuse
Male	2	4.5	8	18.2	10	22.7
Female	10	22.7	24	54.5	34	77.3
Total	12	27.2	32	72.7	44	100.0

THE VICTIMS

It was no surprise that girls were victims at least 77 percent of the time; of all female sexual abuse, white girls outnumbered black girls more than 2:1 (see Table 9–5). Seven of these black children were both physically and sexually abused, and two were raped. Two white children were also raped. In all but two cases of black abuse and four cases of white abuse only one child was victimized.

The introduction of age as a variable also revealed interesting relationships. In sexual abuse, the ages of the victims varied with their race; white girls were increasingly at risk as they aged, with 42 percent of their total sexual abuse occurring during the late adolescent period (fifteen to eighteen years old). On the other hand, younger black children, specifically those between the ages of ten and fourteen, represented 50 percent of the total black abuse. Sexual abuse of boys was extremely rare, with only eight cases of white abuse, evenly divided across age groups, and two confirmed cases of black abuse (one infant and one boy in the group aged ten to fourteen years old).

THE CONTEXT OF ABUSE

Four-fifths of black abuse and two-thirds of white abuse in towns and small cities occurred in the child's home. Three incidents of white abuse occurred in a relative's house and an equal number at a neighbor's. Black households were quite large in these communities, with an average of six members, four of whom were children. Four of the twelve cases were in households with eight children. White households were generally smaller, with an average of four members, two adults and two children.

White sexual abuse occurred 38 percent of the time in step-family homes and 28 percent each in homes headed by a woman and those with both parents, as can be seen in Table 9–6. Inter-estingly, black children were also equally abused in female-headed households and in households with both parents; step-families, however, represented only 17 percent of black sexual abuse. Black children in these communities were not at greater risk in female-headed households (the risk factor was .74).

Caretakers were responsible for 67 percent of all black female sexual abuse and 53 percent of all white female sexual abuse. Five white children were sexually abused by other relatives; four black children and nine white children were abused by neighbors, schoolmates, and so forth. Not surprisingly, males were generally the perpetrators of sexual abuse, with fathers, stepfathers, and the male friends of mothers accounting for the majority of the cases (see Table 9–7). No cases of homosexual abuse of black boys were reported, but 50 percent of the sexual abuse of white

Table 9–6

Percentages of Sexual Abuse in Towns and Small Cities by Type of Household and Race* of Victim

Household Type	Black (N=12)	White (N=32)
Female-headed	41.7	28.1
Both biological parents	41.7	28.1
Father only	—	3.1
Stepfamily	16.7	37.5
Unknown	—	3.1

*$X^2=3.67$; df=4; NS

Table 9–7

Percentages of Perpetrators of Sexual Abuse in Towns and Small
Cities by Race of Victim

Perpetrator	Black	White
Father	41.7 (N=5)	25.0 (N=8)
Both biological parents	—	3.1 (N=1)
Stepfather	16.7 (N=2)	15.6 (N=5)
Stepmother	—	9.4 (N=3)
Grandfather	—	6.3 (N=2)
Uncle	—	6.3 (N=2)
Brother	—	3.1 (N=1)
Male friend	16.7 (N=2)	15.6 (N=5)
Other*	24.9 (N=3)	15.6 (N=5)

*includes cousin, neighbor, female friend, and unknown perpetrator

boys was homosexual; fathers, stepfathers, and grandfathers, as
well as the male friends of the mother, were the perpetrators. The
only incident of female homosexual abuse was perpetrated by a
white stepmother.

THE INJURIES RESULTING FROM ABUSE

One would not expect a large number of physical injuries in
sexual abuse; therefore, it is not surprising that the most frequently noted injuries to sexually abused children were psychological in nature. Abused white boys were recognized in the
caseworkers' reports as having emotional injuries in 63 percent of
the cases, compared to only 29 percent of the reports of white
girls. A positive linear relationship occurred between reported

psychological damage and the age of the child in both black and white abuse. Several children (white children were 2:1 over blacks) had bruises. One black girl contracted venereal disease, and two black girls became pregnant due to the sexual abuse.

DISPOSITION OF CASES

The perpetrator of sexual abuse of black children was removed from the household in one-fourth of the cases (N = 3) and in 22 percent of white sexual abuse cases (N = 7), with an equal distribution across the ages of the children involved. One preadolescent black child was removed from the home; ten (31 percent) white children were removed, six to the homes of relatives, two to foster care, and two to the homes of friends. The perpetrators were criminally charged in only four cases of sexual abuse to black girls, one to a black boy, and in ten cases of sexual abuse to white girls. Two stepfathers, two male friends, and a neighbor were charged with abuse of black children, as were two each of fathers, grandfathers, male friends, and unidentified perpetrators, and one uncle and one stepfather who abused white children.

Sexual Abuse in Urbanized Areas

The total number of children confirmed as having been sexually abused in urbanized areas was small: twenty-two black children, one of whom was a boy, and forty-four white children, ten of whom were boys (see Table 9–8). Seven of these children were raped (three blacks and four whites), and nine (six of whom were white) were both physically and sexually abused.

THE VICTIMS

Sixty-seven percent of sexual abuse in urbanized areas was abuse of white children, and white girls outnumbered boys by a wide margin, as shown in Table 9–8. White girls also greatly outnumbered black girls. Only one black boy was sexually abused. All black abuse and 78 percent of white abuse involved a single

Table 9–8

Sexual Abuse in Urbanized Areas by Race and Sex of Victim

Sex	Black		White		Total	
	N	% of Abuse	N	% of Abuse	N	% of Abuse
Male	1	1.5	10	15.2	11	16.7
Female	21	31.8	34	51.5	55	83.3
Total	22	33.3	44	66.7	66	100.0

victim. An astounding 75 percent of black sexual abuse victimized the first-born child in the family; just over half of white abuse involved the first-born.

Almost 60 percent of white sexual abuse took place during the victim's early teenage years (ages ten to fourteen), but among blacks the incidence was roughly equivalent across all age groups, with a slight peak (33 percent) in the elementary age group (five to nine years old). Although the numbers in all cases were very small, the suggestion of a markedly different age-race relationship in sexual abuse in urbanized areas is notable.

THE CONTEXT OF ABUSE

Thirty percent of all black sexual abuse occurred in households in which the victim was the only child. In black households over-all, the number of children ranged from one to six, and adults numbered one, two, and three in equal proportions. White families had two children more often than one; the range was from one to five. Sexual abuse in urbanized areas most often involved the abuse of one white child who had a sibling and who lived with both biological parents.

Within black families, as shown in Table 9–9, most predominant was abuse in female-headed households (41 percent of black abuse). Only 16 percent of white sexual abuse took place in these households; most of the remaining white abuse was divided equally between households with both biological parents and within stepfamilies.

Table 9–9

Percentages of Sexual Abuse in Urbanized Areas by Type of Household
and Race* of Victim

Household Type	Black (N=22)	White (N=44)
Female–headed	40.9	15.9
Both biological parents	13.6	34.1
Father only	—	9.1
Stepfamily	27.3	36.4
Other**	18.2	4.5

* X^2=11.39; df=4; p=.02

** refers to households in which a grandparent, a foster parent, or
an unknown person is the household head

Most abuse took place in the child's home (78 percent of black
cases, 70 percent of white cases). The remaining sites included a
relative's house, a neighbor's house, outdoors, at school, and in a
public place, such as a theater or church. For both races, no clear
pattern of location occurred, with the exception that a greater
number of incidents among white families involved repeated
abuse that took place in a variety of settings.

It is not surprising that fathers, stepfathers, male friends, uncles, and brothers were the main perpetrators of sexual abuse, as
shown in Table 9–10. Two cases of homosexual abuse occurred
among black families; one was perpetrated by a male friend on his
girlfriend's son, the other was a mother who abused her daughter.
Among white families, fathers were the abusers in over one-fourth
of the abuse and, interestingly, they sexually abused their sons,
not their daughters, in three of the thirteen cases. In all, there
were at least four cases of white male homosexual abuse but no
cases of white female homosexual abuse. Both parents were involved in the sexual abuse of their sons in three instances of white
abuse and of their daughters in two cases. In summary, caretakers

Table 9–10

Percentages of Perpetrators of Sexual Abuse in Urbanized Areas
by Race of Victim

Perpetrator	Black	White
Father	9.5 (N=2)	29.5 (N=13)
Mother	4.8 (N=1)	—
Both biological parents	4.8 (N=1)	11.4 (N=5)
Stepfather	23.8 (N=5)	20.5 (N=9)
Uncle	9.5 (N=2)	6.8 (N=3)
Aunt	—	2.3 (N=1)
Brother	9.5 (N=2)	4.5 (N=2)
Male friend	14.3 (N=3)	13.6 (N=6)
Unknown	9.5 (N=2)	—
Other*	14.3 (N=3)	11.4 (N=5)

*
includes foster father, neighbor, stranger, and unidentified
perpetrator

were responsible for two-thirds of white abuse; among blacks,
abuse was spread more evenly across categories of caretaker
(43 percent), other relative (17 percent), and "others" (29 percent).

THE INJURIES RESULTING FROM ABUSE

Fifty-nine percent of the black children were not injured, according to the investigators; however, only 25 percent of white
children were uninjured. More than two-thirds of the white girls,
most of whom were preadolescents, were noted to have suffered

from psychological injury; half the white boys suffered likewise, according to the narrative reports. Only one-third of the black girls were reported to have been injured psychologically.

Interestingly, white children received bruises four times more often than black children. Five black girls, four white boys, and two white girls received cuts. Among black girls, the number of injuries was greater in the younger age groups; no injuries were reported among the four teenage girls, and no physical injuries were mentioned in two of the five preadolescents. The pattern was quite different among white girls; notation of injuries, especially psychological injury, increased with age. At least four black and four white girls became pregnant, and three black girls contracted a venereal disease.

DISPOSITION OF CASES

Twenty percent of the sexually abused black children were removed, at least temporarily, from their homes to the home of a relative, 30 percent were put into a foster home, and the remainder were left in the home. Among white children, 31 percent were placed with relatives, and only 8 percent were placed in foster care. Four other white children (10 percent) were removed from the home but the record did not indicate where they were placed.

Twice the proportion of black children as white were referred for a psychological examination or evaluation following the sexual abuse incident, and two-thirds were medically examined, whereas only half the white children were so evaluated.

In all, at the time that the narrative reports were sent to the central registry, the perpetrator had been removed from the household in five black cases (one case each of a stepfather, an uncle, a male friend, a teacher [in which case the child was relocated], and an unknown perpetrator) and in eleven cases of white sexual abuse (five fathers, two stepfathers, two brothers, one uncle, and one male friend). Criminal charges were brought (or were in process) against the perpetrator in three black cases (14 percent) and in fifteen white cases (34 percent). The perpetrators criminally charged in black cases were an uncle, a male friend, and an unknown perpetrator; the perpetrators of white abuse were fathers (N = 8), stepfathers (N = 2), and one each of an uncle, a male friend, a brother, and a stranger. One perpetrator of a white child was unidentified.

Summary

It was expected that girls would be more frequent victims of sexual abuse than boys, but it was surprising that, overall, at least one boy was reported for every four girls. However, the proportion of boys to girls was directly related to both race and community size. The proportion of abuse of black boys (30 percent) to girls was by far the greatest in rural areas. In urbanized areas, on the other hand, only one boy was included in twenty-two reports of sexually abused black children. The proportion of white boys to girls was relatively consistent across communities.

Sexually abused children were likely to be older in areas outside large cities. Urban children were reported at younger ages, due to the large number of hospital reports of black children. The modal age for sexual abuse in general was in the group of children aged ten to fourteen, although white teenagers (fifteen to eighteen) were most frequently abused in towns and small cities and black preschoolers in the urbanized areas. These age-community relationships, however, were not statistically significant, as they had been for black physical abuse.

The modal household, in all communities, had two children, the eldest of whom was the abuse victim. In all communities, both black and white children were at great risk for sexual abuse if they lived in stepfamilies. White children who lived with both of their original parents were at greater risk only in rural areas. The proportion of sexually abused black children living in female-headed households was greater than that of other household types, although in midsized communities abuse was just as frequent in families with both biological parents. In fact, only in these communities were black children not at heightened risk in female-headed households; white children in female-headed households, on the other hand, were at especially great risk in towns and small cities. Nonetheless, the relationship between household type and community size was not significant for either race, as it had been for white physically abused children.

Related to these household patterns, the black child's stepfather was the most frequent perpetrator, except in midsized communities, where the child's own father accounted for a greater proportion of abuse. Among white children, fathers and stepfathers were frequent sexual abusers, regardless of the size of the community in which the victims lived. The male friend of the black child's mother was the abuser in equal proportions across communities. In cases of white abuse, the male friends accounted for a greater proportion of abuse in midsized communities than elsewhere. Although prevalent in all locations, the highest proportion of incestuous abuse occurred in rural areas. These areas also had the greatest variety of perpetrators and the highest proportion of homosexual abuse, with the latter involving boys far more often than girls. On the other hand, urbanized areas were the context for more rapes than elsewhere.

Unlike the characteristics of the actual incidents of abuse themselves, differences related to the disposition of sexual abuse cases and the size of the community met tests of statistical significance. For example, in white abuse, the disposition of the child and the size of the community were highly related. Almost half of the children in the larger cities were removed, at least temporarily; in towns and small cities, almost 30 percent were removed; and in rural areas, 20 percent were relocated ($X^2 = 20.12$; df $= 8$; p $= .00$). Among black children, the relationship was not statistically significant. For both black and white children, a significant relationship existed between medical evaluation and community size. White children were evaluated in over 25 percent of the cases of rural abuse and 50 percent of the cases of urban abuse but in only 12 percent of those in the midsized communities. Medical evaluations of black children followed the same patterns but were much higher in frequency than for white children.

As discussed above, the configurations of abuse victims, reporters, and perpetrators tended to vary only moderately with the size of the community and were not significant statistically. The results of this study lend support to the hypothesis that sexual abuse, unlike physical abuse, is not strongly related to external sociological conditions. However, the literature also stresses that the covert nature of sexual abuse makes it less visible to surveillance and reporting. Its apparent acceptability in certain cultures may also reduce the numbers of reports from those areas, masking a true sociological relationship. It is interesting, for example, to speculate on the caseworkers' notations of excessive alcohol use in 42 percent of the black cases in towns and small cities, compared to 5 and 14 percent in rural and urbanized areas, respectively. Although such large differences were not found among white perpetrators, more abuse related to alcohol was found in urban places (28 percent) than in rural areas (16 percent) or midsized communities (13 percent). These differences must be treated cautiously, however, because their notation was dependent upon the caseworker's narrative style. However, they do suggest that social and cultural factors may indeed influence the incidence of sexual child abuse. There is clearly a great deal to learn.

Epilogue

Eight years ago, the Alabama Law Institute held a symposium on child abuse and neglect. At that conference, the director of the Bureau of Family and Children Services, Louise Pittman, described the child abuse Central Registry in the Department of Pensions and Security. She said:

> Frankly, we have computer trouble. We have never been able to computerize the reports. We are stacking them all over the place. . . . We are looking this year at our getting on the national system. We have it out there but they have a hard time dealing with us on what they can transfer from our records to the national data. We are deeply sympathetic with the need for valid data . . . [and] we hope to try to convert to their system, if we have the manpower to do it. This will get Alabama at least in the national scene and will give us retrievable data more quickly. (1977, p. 61)

That was in 1977. There is no computerized system yet, and there is no way to update these 1982–83 data without replicating the study as we conducted it, an extremely costly and inefficient means of tracking child abuse victims or of calculating annual incidence rates. Therefore, as a means of evaluating the changes that may have occurred in the reporting of child abuse or its characteristics, in the fall of 1985 the supervisors of DPS protective services in the twenty-five sampled counties were asked to comment on the status of their current services and on the characteristics of child abuse, as they perceived them, in their respective counties. Two county supervisors, both from rural counties in the middle-eastern part of the state, did not participate in the survey.

These supervisors reported that, since 1982, the number of investigations by DPS caseworkers had increased by 28 percent to a total of 28,000 in 1984. In that same period, DPS had been subjected to several hiring freezes, which have not only prevented a growth in the numbers of caseworkers commensurate with the increase in the number of reports, but which have also prohibited caseworker replacement in the event of resignations and retirements. Since 1982, there had been a loss of at least twenty investigators across the twenty-three counties. All counties had lost protective caseworkers, and some have had to transfer workers from adult services or foster care services in order to deal with staff attrition. In one county, the supervisor herself made investigations.

On the average, each caseworker made 98 investigations of abuse and neglect per year, with a range of 15 to 300 and an average gain since 1982 of 67 cases. In addition, investigators in all but three counties also carried an ongoing protective services caseload averaging 71 children, with a range of 35 to 170. The national "ideal" is a more manageable 40 cases per worker. One county supervisor admitted that these ongoing cases were necessarily "culled" to keep caseloads at a manageable number. Others agreed that cases were no longer carried very long because there was time only for investigations, not for follow-up.

An inescapable result of understaffing was that all counties except one were seriously backlogged in their investigations of child abuse and neglect reports. One supervisor, who estimated that at least 400 cases were in some respect incomplete, remarked, "We all have to go to bed with that reality every night." Another, who was 66 reports behind, similarly remarked that "These uninvestigated reports are what give each of us constant nightmares." One urban county had reports from 1984 that had not yet been investigated; that county's total backlog was more than 1,000 reports. The huge number, the supervisor explained, was directly related to severe understaffing in combination with the four or five acute emergencies reported each day, which reduced their protective services to that of a "crisis unit."

Staffing shortages also affected clerical effectiveness. Many counties reported that they were months (one county was a year) behind in dictation of the investigation summaries, a prerequisite to a case's reassignment for follow-up protective services.

The county supervisors were asked their perceptions of the current comprehensiveness and accuracy of the reporting networks in their counties. All but one supervisor responded that reporting had increased since 1982, although they thought that the characteristics of abuse incidents themselves had not significantly changed. As was true in 1982, most supervisors estimated that well over half of the reports they received were unfounded and partially blamed inadequate definitions of abuse. Most counties found "vindictive" and "malicious" reports to be a problem, especially from couples who were fighting custody arrangements. In general, however, and across the counties, friends and relatives were considered reliable reporters, "people who care." One-quarter of all the reports were considered serious and, ideally, would be investigated immediately; these reports were characterized by severe injury and/or abandonment.

The quality of reporting sources in most counties was erratic. For example, a common experience was for one school system or hospital within a county to report well, another to make no reports ("because they will get into trouble if they do"). Great variability also occurred in the seasonal patterns of some reporting groups: in one county, reports escalate in September when the schools reenter the reporting network; another county experiences an increase each spring when that county's schools make the bulk of their reports, "turning over the summer surveillance to DPS."

As a rule, physicians were the most disappointing of any professional reporting group, although several supervisors observed that some doctors, especially the younger ones, were "wonderful" about reporting. One supervisor said that doctors in her county "just refuse to get involved, no matter how much we stress the importance of reporting." A supervisor from a rural county suggested that physicians' failure to report was due to "family loyalty."

According to the supervisors, hospitals were a good source of reports, especially if they had a social worker or a nursing staff trained in child abuse detection. One supervisor commented, however, that if anyone made a report from a nearby middle class hospital, "they would be fired tomorrow."

The general consensus was that professionals and the public were better informed about child abuse today and that the increase in reports reflected heightened sensitivity. Only one supervisor thought that the increase in reports indicated an increase in the actual amount of abuse. The supervisors also thought that the type of abuse they were investigating reliably reflected the type of abuse that exists beyond the surveillance-reporting network— with the strong exception of sexual abuse. Almost all supervisors agreed that they do not receive enough sexual abuse reports, due, they believed, to a strong reluctance by reporters to get involved. In addition, they felt that, in rural places especially, much sexual abuse occurred that they suspected to be multigenerational and, therefore, accepted. Just one supervisor, from a predominantly black and rural county, thought that the public was not sufficiently aware of physical abuse, in spite of DPS outreach efforts, and she therefore suspected that they were missing many cases.

Morale in the county offices was low. One supervisor, in trying to explain the indifference of many state legislators to the financial hardships at DPS, remarked, "People just can't, or won't, absorb how awful it is!" It is hard to imagine a more difficult job than the daily intrusion into families to determine whether they are, in fact, abusing their children and, if they are, to then vainly search for services and resources to intervene on behalf of a child. Twice in the past two years, county offices had been required to restrict all travel and to leave the office only for emergency reports. The urgency of a report is obviously hard to assess, inasmuch as the decision must be based only on a telephone call. No follow-up services were rendered during these travel-restricted intervals. It was not only the horror of abuse and the lack of services, however, that were so demoralizing, according to one supervisor; she said that the most shocking thing about her job was the frequency with which people will lie to her and resist her help. "Nine out of ten perpetrators, family members, even the victims," she said, "will quickly and easily lie. They develop outlandish fantasies to explain the injuries."

Summary

The child protection movement in the state of Alabama, as in the nation, is at an important crossroads. With mandated reporting, central registries, "hot lines," and media coverage, the increase in reported cases has overwhelmed available resources. As described in chapters 1 and 2, little is known about the causes or characteristics of child abuse; even less is understood about treatment for the abusers or the abused. Professionals continue to be divided, as they have been since the early days of the SPCC, between child abuse as a social welfare issue and as a legal issue, the former position based upon the theory of family dysfunction and the latter on a theory of criminal wrongdoing. At the core of the controversy is the lack of available evidence in support of either theoretical position. Little evidence exists that family therapy is effective against recurrence of abuse and virtually no evidence that imprisonment of the perpetrator deters future episodes, either in a specific case or in general.

Absolutely essential to resolution of this conflict is the development of a solid knowledge base. Information gathered prospectively and in detail is the only way to understand the characteristics of child abuse and their relationship to social and economic conditions over time. The first step is to fund the design and implementation of a mechanism for collecting information. Last year more than 28,000 cases of abuse and neglect were reported to the state registry (the total number is well over 130,000 reports since 1975), and this extraordinary wealth of information is only stored away. Within that data base are hidden the answers to such questions as: What is the relationship between the recent recession and the incidence of abuse? What is the relationship between perpetrator characteristics and multiple reports or recurrence of abuse? How effective are various intervention strategies—for example, have there been repeated episodes of abuse by perpetrators arrested and imprisoned, or by perpetrators who attended parenting classes? Are the child victims of ten years ago the perpetrators of abuse today? Or are they today's criminals?

We have lost ten years of opportunity. Let us stop at that.

APPENDIX A

Department of Pensions and Security Form 959

STATE OF ALABAMA
DEPARTMENT OF PENSIONS AND SECURITY
REPORT OF SUSPECTED CASE OF CHILD ABUSE/NEGLECT

FORMERLY PSD-159

| Co. No. | Rec'd in State Office |

☐ ABUSE ☐ NEGLECT

| County Name | PSD Case Number |

SECTION I — AUTHORITY

ACCORDING TO ACT NO. 563, ACTS OF ALABAMA 1965 AS AMENDED BY ACT NO. 725, REGULAR SESSION 1967 AND ACT NO. 1124, REGULAR SESSION 1975, NOW CODIFIED AS CODE OF ALABAMA, 1975, SECTION 26-14-1 THROUGH 26-14-13. A WRITTEN REPORT IS REQUIRED BY STATUTE. PERSONS REPORTING ARE REQUESTED TO FILL OUT IN TRIPLICATE AS MUCH INFORMATION AS IS KNOWN TO THEM.

SECTION II — VICTIMS

First Name	MI	Last Name	Sex	Race	Date of Birth

SECTION III - PARENT(S)/CUSTODIAN

(Father's) First Name	MI	Last Name		Race	Date of Birth
Street Address	City	State	Zip Code	Marital Status	Telephone No.
(Mother's) First Name	MI	Last Name		Race	Date of Birth
Street Address	City	State	Zip Code	Marital Status	Telephone No.
(Custodian's) First Name	MI	Last Name		Race	Date of Birth

SECTION V -- ALLEGED PERPETRATOR(S)

First Name	MI	Last Name	Sex	Race	Date of Birth

Address		City	State	Zip Code	Relationship to Victim

SECTION VI — INCIDENT

Time	Place	Date	Name of person reporting	Relationship to Victim

Case Reported To: ☐ Police ☐ Sheriff ☐ DPS ☐ Other (specify)

Description of Incident:

Result:

Previous incident(s) of abuse/neglect involving child(ren) or perpetrator(s). Describe:

Signature of person completing form   Title, Agency, or Relationship to Victim(s)

SECTION VII – DPS DISPOSITION

Summary Removal Required:
☐ Yes ☐ No

☐ Founded
☐ Unfounded ☐ Undetermined

Where placed if removed:
☐ Shelter ☐ Relative ☐ Foster Home

Other Services (specify)

Date Rec'd in County DPS	Date investigation started

Worker's Signature

PSD-BFC-959
05/81
Supersedes all previous editions
of PSD-159

DISTRIBUTION: White Copy -- State Office
Yellow Copy – County Office
Pink Copy – State Office

APPENDIX B
Confirmed Abuse Data
Collection Form

```
┌─────────────────────────────────────────┐
│ COUNTY_____PSD CASE #_____          │
└─────────────────────────────────────────┘
```

┌──────────────┐
│ II. Victims │
└──────────────┘

| Child 1   < 2 Years
Sex:___ (1) Male (2) Female
Race:___ (1)Black (2)White (3)Other
Year of Birth:_____
| Child 2   _____ mos.
Sex:___ (1)Male (2) Female
Race:___ (1)Black (2)White (3)Other
Year of Birth:_____
| _____ mos.
| Child 3
Sex:___ (1)Male (2) Female
Race:___ (1)Black (2)White (3)Other
Year of Birth:_____
| _____ mos.

Total # of child victims_____

┌──────────────┐
│ III. Parents │
└──────────────┘
Father
Race: _____ (1) Black (2) White (3) Other
Year of Birth: _____
Marital Status:___(1)Married (2)Divorced
                    (3)Never Married
                    (4)Separated (5)Widowed
                    (6)Unknown
Same last name as victim?___(1)Yes (2)No (3)Unknown

_____
(City)
Mother
Race: _____ (1) Black (2) White (3) Other
Year of Birth: _____
Marital Status:___(1)Married (2)Divorced
                    (3)Never Married
                    (4)Separated (5)Widowed
                    (6)Unknown
Same last name as victim? ___ (1)Yes (2)No (3)Unknown

_____
(City)

Custodian
Sex:____ (1)Male (2)Female
Race:___ (1)Black (2)White (3)Other
Year of Birth:___
Marital Status:___ (1)Married (2)Divor
                    (3)Never Married
                    (4)Separated (5)Widowed
                    (6)Unknown
Relationship to victim:___
                    (1)Grandparent
                    (2)Aunt (3)Uncle
                    (4)Friend
                    (5)Legal Guardian
                    (6)Sibling (7)other
                    (8)Unknown
                    (9)Foster Parent

148

```
┌─────────────────────────────────┐
│        IV. OTHER CHILDREN        │
│     (NOT listed under VICTIMS)   │
└─────────────────────────────────┘
              Child 1
```
Sex:___ (1)Male (2)Female
Race:___ (1)Black (2)White (3)Other
Year of Birth:_____
Relationship to victim:___
          (1)Brother
          (2)Sister
          (3)Cousin
          (4)Not related
          (5)Step brother
          (6)Step sister
          (7)Other
          (8)Unknown

              Child 2
Sex:___ (1) Male (2) Female
Race:___ (1) Black (2) White (3) Other
Year of Birth:___
Relationship to victim:___ (1)Brother (2)Sister
                           (3)Cousin ((4)Not related
                           (5)Step brother
                           (6)Step sister
                           (7)Other (8)Unknown
              Child 3
Sex:___ (1) Male (2) Female
Race:___ (1) Black (2) White (3) Other
Year of Birth:___
Relationship to victim:___ (1)Brother (2)Sister
                           (3)Cousin (4)Not related
                           (5)Step brother
                           (6)Step sister
                           (7)Other (8) Unknown

```
┌─────────────────────────┐
│    V. PERPETRATOR(S)     │
└─────────────────────────┘
       Perpetrator 1
```
Sex:___ (1) Male (2) Female
Race:___ (1)Black (2)White (3)Other
Year of Birth:___
Relationship to victim:___ (1)Father (2)Mother
                           (3)Step father (4)Step mother
                           (5)Grandfather (6)Grandmother
                           (7)Aunt (8)Uncle
                           (9)Friend(male)
                           (10)Friend(female)
                           (11)Legal Guardian
                           (12)Brother (13)Sister
                           (14)Babysitter (male)
                           (15)Babysitter (female)
                           (16)Foster father
                           (17)Foster mother
                           (18)Adoptive father
                           (19)Adoptive mother
                           (20)Teacher (21)Unknown
                           (22)Other

City:_____
State:_____ (See State Listing)

       Perpetrator 2
Sex:___ (1) Male (2) Female
Race:___ (1)Black (2)White (3)Other
Year of Birth:___
Relationship to victim:___
                           (1)Father (2)Mother
                           (3)Step father (4)Step mother
                           (5)Grandfather (6)Grandmother
                           (7)Aunt (8)Uncle
                           (9)Friend (male)
                           (10)Friend (female)
                           (11)Legal guardian
                           (12)Brother (13)Sister
                           (14)Babysitter (male)
                           (15)Babysitter (female)
                           (16)Foster father
                           (17)Foster mother
                           (18)Adoptive father
                           (19)Adoptive mother
                           (20)Teacher
                           (21)Unknown
                           (22)Other
City:_____
State:_____ (See State Listing)

Time:____   **VI. INCIDENT**
            (1)Morning (6:01 thru 11:59)
            (2)Afternoon(noon thru 5:59)
            (3)Evening (6:00 thru 9:00)
            (4)After 9 P.M., before 6 A.M.

Place:____   (1)Own house (2) Relative's
            house (3) Neighbor's house
            (4) Outdoors (5) School
            (6) Public place (7) Church
            (8) More than one incident/more
            than one place (9) Other
Date: ___/___/___
More than one date?_____

                        Relationship to victim of person reporting:____
                                                    (1)Mother (2)Father
                                                    (3)Grandparent (4)Uncle
                                                    (5)Aunt (6)Friend/neighbor
                                                    (7)Legal Guardian (8)Sibling
                                                    (9)Self (10)Police (11)Sheriff
                                                    (12)Clergy (13)Social Worker/
                                                    Community Worker (14)Education
                                                    (15)Physician (16)Other
                                                    (17)Unknown (18)Hospital(excluding
                                                    physicians)

_____ Case reported to:___
                                                    (1)Police (2)Sheriff (3)DPS
_____   (4)Other (specify)_____
                         Description of Incident:___
                                                    (1)Physical abuse (2)Sexual
                                                    abuse (3)Both physical and
                                                    sexual abuse (4)Emotional Abuse
_____ Result: (5)Rape
                                          _____   (1)neurological effects
                                          _____   (2)burns
                                          _____   (3)fractures
                                          _____   (4)bruises
                                          _____   (5)cuts
                                          _____   (6)psychological effects
                                          _____   (7)death
                                          _____   (8)hospitalization

_____

                                    VII. Disposition
Following the incident of abuse:
                                    NO   YES
    Was the child medically treated ___   ___   ___
    Was the child removed from the
        household?   ___   ___   Where?_____
    Was the perpetrator removed?   ___   ___   Where?_____
    Was the perpetrator arrested or
        criminally charged?   ___   ___   ___
    Psychiatric or psychological
        evaluation   ___   ___   ___
    Was there a home visit?   ___   ___   ___

Household type: Family Characteristics
(1)Biological Parents   (4)Step-family
(2)Female-headed   (5)Foster family
(3)Father only   (6)Other
How many adults (>18 yrs) live in same household?   _____
How many children (< 18 yrs) live in same household?   _____
How many (natural,step,adoptive) siblings does the   _____
  victim have?
What is the birth order of the victim?_____ out
of_____.   (1st,2nd,3rd,etc.)
   (Total)
How long has child lived in this house?
____/____ All life _____
yrs. mos.

Employment

	Perpetrator	Mother	Father	*Head of Household
homemaker				
chronic (1 yr) unemployed				
temporarily unemployed				
regular employment				
occasional employment				
disabled				
student				
retired				

*if other than mother or father

Social & Medical History

	Perpetrator	Mother	Father	*Head of Household
history of mental illness				
mental retardation				
criminal activity				
jail record				
alcoholism				
drug use				
previous marriages				
previous child abuse/physical				
previous child neglect				
previous sexual abuse of child				

SES: From the narrative record, would you describe the socioeconomic
status of this household as:
_____ (1)Professional - upper middle class
_____ (2)Professional/managerial - middle class
_____ (3)Working class - lower middle class
_____ (4)Labor/blue collar
_____ (5)Unemployed
_____ (6)ADC
_____ (7)Receiving disability
_____ (8)Don't know

How is the child described by the social worker:

intelligence: _____ retarded   _____ not mentioned
                     _____ normal
                     _____ very bright

appearance: _____ not attractive   _____ not mentioned
                     _____ normal range
                     _____ very attractive
                     _____ physically disabled/disfigured. Explain_____

academic record: _____ does not go to school _____ not mentioned
                     _____ failing
                     _____ average
                     _____ very good

behavior record: _____ delinquent/troublesome _____ not mentioned
                     _____ normal
                     _____ outstanding

physical maturity: _____ slow/below normal   _____ not mentioned
                     _____ normal
                     _____ precocious

sexuality: _____ normal   _____ not mentioned
                     _____ seductive but not active sexually
                     _____ active sexually

EDUCATION:
   Mother: _____
               (1)Elementary School only
               (2)< High School
               (3)High School
               (4)Some College
               (5)College
               (6)> College
               (7)DK

   Father: _____
               (1)Elementary School only
               (2)< High School
               (3)High School
               (4)Some College
               (5)College
               (6)> College
               (7)DK

COMMENTS:

References

American Humane Society. 1978. *National analysis of the incidence and severity of child abuse reporting.* Denver: The Association.

American Medical Association Council on Scientific Affairs. 1985. AMA diagnostic and treatment guidelines concerning child abuse and neglect. *Journal of the American Medical Association* 254:796–800.

Aries, P. 1962. *Centuries of childhood.* New York: Vantage.

Bagley, C. 1984. Child sexual abuse: Annotated bibliography of studies 1978–1984. *Calgary: Rehabilitation and Health Monographs* 12. Calgary: University of Calgary Press.

Baker, C. 1978. Preying on playgrounds: The sex exploitation of children in pornography and prostitution. *Pepperdine Law Review* 5:809–56.

Baldwin, J. A., and J. E. Oliver. 1975. Epidemiology and family characteristics of severely abused children. *British Journal of Preventive and Social Medicine* 29:205–21.

Brant, R. S., and V. B. Tisza. 1977. The sexually misused child. *American Journal of Orthopsychiatry* 47:80.

Bullough, V. 1976. *Sexual variance in society and history.* New York: Wiley.

Burgess, A. 1982. Research on the use of children in pornography. *Executive summary report to National Center on Child Abuse and Neglect.* Washington, D.C.

———, ed. 1984. *Child pornography and sex rings.* Lexington, Mass.: Lexington Books.

Butler, A. 1954. *Portrait of Josephine Butler.* London: Faber & Faber.

Daniel, J. H., R. L. Hampton, and E. H. Newberger. 1983. Child abuse and accidents in black families: A controlled comparative study. *American Journal of Orthopsychiatry* 53:645–53.

de Mause, L. 1974. *The history of childhood.* New York: Psychohistory Press.

Department of Health and Human Services. 1981. *National study of the incidence and severity of child abuse and neglect.* (DHHS Publication No. 81-30325). Washington, D.C.: U.S. Government Printing Office.

Department of Health, Education, and Welfare. 1977. *Child abuse and neglect programs: Practice and theory.* (DHEW Publication No. ADM 77-344). Washington, D.C.: U.S. Government Printing Office.

Dillingham, J., and E. Melmed. 1982. Child pornography: A study of the social sexual abuse of children. *Executive summary report to the National Center on Child Abuse and Neglect.* Washington, D.C.

Elmer, E. 1966. Hazards in determining child abuse. *Child Welfare* 45:28–33.

Finkelhor, D. 1979. *Sexually victimized children.* New York: Free Press.

———. 1984. *Child sexual abuse: New theory in research.* New York: Macmillan.

Fontana, V. J., D. Donovan, and R. J. Wong. 1963. The maltreatment syndrome of children. *New England Journal of Medicine* 269:1389.

Foster, H., and A. Freed. 1964. Offense against the family. *University of Missouri K.C. Law Review* 32:35–45.

Garbarino, J., and B. A. Crouter. 1978. A note on the problem of construct validity in assessing the usefulness of child maltreatment report data. *American Journal of Public Health* 68:598–600.

Gelles, R. J. 1973. Child abuse as psychopathology: A sociological critique and reformulation. *American Journal of Orthopsychiatry* 43:611–21.

———. 1975. The social construction of child abuse. *American Journal of Orthopsychiatry* 45:363–71.

———. 1980. Violence in the family: A review of research in the 70's. *Journal of Marriage and the Family* 42:873–85.

Gil, D. G. 1969. Physical abuse of children: Findings and implications of a nationwide survey. *Pediatrics* 44:857–64.

———. 1970. *Violence against children: Physical child abuse in the U.S.* Cambridge, Mass.: Harvard University Press.

Greenberg, N. 1979. The epidemiology of childhood sexual abuse. *Pediatric Annals* 8:289–99.

Haeberle, E. 1977. Historical roots of sexual oppression. In *The sexually oppressed,* ed. H. J. Gochros. New York: Association Press.

Hampton, R. L., and E. H. Newberger. 1985. Child abuse incidence and reporting by hospitals: Significance of severity, class and race. *American Journal of Public Health* 75:56–59.

Herman, J. 1984. The seduction theory controversy. *Journal of the American Medical Women's Association* 39(5):68–169, 172.

Hicks, D. J. 1980. Rape: Sexual assault. *American Journal of Obstetrics* and *Gynecology* 137:931–35.

James, J. 1977. Early sexual experience and prostitution. *American Journal of Psychiatry* 134:1381–85.

Jason, J., and N. D. Andereck. 1983. Fatal child abuse in Georgia: The epidemiology of severe physical child abuse. *Child Abuse and Neglect* 7:1–9.

Jason, J., N. D. Andereck, J. Marks, and C. W. Tyler, Jr. 1982. Child abuse in Georgia: A method to evaluate risk factors and reporting bias. *American Journal of Public Health* 72:1353–58.

Jason, J., S. L. Williams, A. Burton, and R. Rochat. 1982. Epidemiologic differences between sexual and physical child abuse. *Journal of the American Medical Association* 247:3344–48.

Jones, E., ed. 1959. *Sigmund Freud: Collected papers*. New York: Basic Books.

Kempe, C. H., and R. E. Helfer, eds. 1972. *Helping the battered child and his family*. Philadelphia: J. B. Lippincott.

Kempe, C. H., F. N. Silverman, B. F. Steele, W. Droegemueller, and H. K. Silver. 1962. The battered-child syndrome. *Journal of the American Medical Association* 181:17–24.

Korbin, J. E. 1981. *Child abuse and neglect: Cross-cultural perspectives*. Berkeley and Los Angeles: University of California Press.

Kramer, D., and D. J. Jason. 1982. Sexually abused children and sexually transmitted diseases. *Review of Infectious Diseases* 4:S883–90.

Lauer, B., E. Ten Broeck, and M. Grossman. 1974. Battered child syndrome: Review of 130 patients with controls. *Pediatrics* 54:67–70.

Lustig, N., J. W. Dresser, S. W. Spellman, and T. B. Murray. 1966. Incest: A family group survival pattern. *Archives of General Psychiatry* 14:31–40.

McCarthy, B. J., R. W. Rochat, B. Cundiff, P. A. Gould, and S. Quave. 1981. Child abuse registry in Georgia: Three years of experience. *Southern Medical Journal* 74:11–16.

Manchester, A. H. 1979. The law of incest in England and Wales. *Child Abuse and Neglect* 3:679.

Mead, M. 1968. Incest. *International encyclopedia of social sciences*, vol. 7. New York: Macmillan and Free Press.

Mohr, N. W., R. E. Turner, and M. B. Jerry. 1964. *Pedophilia and exhibitionism*. Toronto: University of Toronto Press.

Mrazek, P. B., and C. H. Kempe. 1981. *Sexually abused children and their families*. Ontario: Pergerman Press.

Newberger, E. H., and J. H. Daniel. 1976. Knowledge and epidemiology of child abuse: A critical review of concepts. *Pediatric Annals* 5:15–21.

Newberger, E. H., and J. N. Hyde. 1975. Child abuse: Principles and implications of current pediatric practice. *Pediatric Clinics of North America* 22:695.

O'Brien, J. E. 1971. Violence in divorce prone families. *Journal of Marriage and the Family* 33:692–98.

Parke, R. D., and C. W. Collmer. 1975. Child abuse: An interdisciplinary analysis. In *Review of child development research*, ed. E. M. Hetherington, 5:509–90. Chicago: University of Chicago Press.

Pelton, L. H. 1978. The myths of classlessness in child abuse cases. *American Journal of Orthopsychiatry* 48:569–76.

Peters, J. 1976. Children who are victims of sexual assault. *American Journal of Psychotherapy* 30:398–421.

Peters, J. J., and R. L. Sadoff. 1970. Clinical observations on child molesters. *Human Sexuality,* November.

Pittman, L. 1977. Problems of child abuse and neglect. In University of Alabama Law Center, Alabama Law Institute, *Child abuse and neglect: A community approach.* University, Ala.: The University of Alabama.

Radzinowicz, L. 1948. *History of English criminal law.* New York: Macmillan.

Russell, D. 1983. Incidence and prevalence of intrafamilial and extrafamilial sexual abuse of female children. *Child Abuse and Neglect* 7:133–46.

———. 1984. *Sexual exploitation: Rape, child sexual abuse, and sexual harassment.* Beverly Hills, Calif.: Sage Press.

Schultz, L. G. 1980. *The sexual-victimology of youth.* Springfield, Ill.: Charles C. Thomas.

Silverman, F. N. 1953. The roentgen manifestations of unrecognized skeletal trauma in infants. *American Journal of Roentgenology* 69:413–26.

———. 1972. Unrecognized trauma in infants, the battered-child syndrome, and the syndrome of Ambroise Tardieu. *Radiology* 104:337–53.

Starbuck, G. W., N. Krantzler, K. Forbes, and V. Barnes. 1984. Child abuse and neglect on Oahu, Hawaii: Description and analysis of four purported risk factors. *Journal of Developmental and Behavioral Pediatrics* 5:55–59.

Steele, B. J., and C. B. Pollock. 1974. A psychiatric study of parents who abuse infants and small children. In *The battered child*, ed. R. E. Helfer and C. H. Kempe, 80–133. Chicago: University of Chicago Press.

Straus, M., R. Gelles, and S. Steinmetz. 1980. *Behind closed doors: Violence in the American family.* Garden City, N.Y.: Doubleday.

Summit, R., and J. Kryso. 1978. Sexual abuse of children: A clinical spectrum. *American Journal of Orthopsychiatry* 48:237–51.

Tyler, T. 1982. *Child pornography.* Paper presented at the Fourth Annual International Congress on Child Abuse and Neglect, Paris, France.

Weinberg, S. K. 1955. *Incest behavior.* New York: Citadel Press.

Weissberg, M. 1983. *Dangerous secrets: Maladaptive responses to stress.* New York: W. W. Norton.

West, D. 1974. Thoughts on sex law reforms. In *Crime, criminology and public policy,* ed. R. Hood, 469–88. New York: Free Press.

White, S. T., F. A. Loda, and D. L. Ingram. 1983. Sexually transmitted diseases in sexually abused children. *Pediatrics* 72:16–21.

Index

Alabama, demography, 15; sample county rates, 75–76; statewide rates of physical abuse, 77; statewide rates of sexual abuse, 89
Alabama Child Abuse Act (1977), 30
American Humane Society (AHS), 10

Child Abuse and Neglect Reporting Law (Alabama), 28–30
Child prostitution, 5, 6, 7, 25
Child Protective Services, 11
Children's Bureau, Department of Labor, 10
Community size, definition of, 15; physical abuse reporting and, 52–62; sexual abuse reporting and, 62–64; comparison of, and reporting, 64–71; comparison of, and abuse characteristics: physical abuse, 118–22; sexual abuse, 138–40. *See also* Rural areas, Towns and small cities, Urbanized areas
Context of abuse
in physical abuse: statewide, 81–85; in rural areas, 100–102; in towns and small cities, 108–09; in urbanized areas, 113–15; summary, 119–20
in sexual abuse: statewide, 92–93; in rural areas, 126; in towns and small cities, 130–31; in urban areas, 134–36; summary, 138

Definitions of child abuse, 1, 2; problems with, 1–8, 9, 41–42, 48. *See also* Laws

Department of Pensions and Security, 28–29, 141; Central Registry, 29–30, 36
Disposition of cases
in physical abuse: statewide, 87–88; in rural areas, 105–06; in towns and small cities, 110–11; in urbanized areas, 117–18
in sexual abuse: statewide, 95–96; in rural areas, 129; in towns and small cities, 133; in urbanized areas, 137–38

Epidemiology, problems in, 7, 22, 23–24
Exhibitionism, 4
Exploitation, 5

Family size. *See* Context of abuse
Family type, 13, 45, 46. *See also* Context of abuse

History of child abuse, physical, 9–14; sexual, 17–25
Homosexual abuse, 3. *See also* Incest
Household type. *See* Context of abuse

Incest, 3, 4, 6, 18, 19, 20, 21, 22, 25; risk factors in, 18
Incidence of abuse: national, 11, 12, 43; in Alabama sample counties, 76
of physical abuse in Alabama: statewide, 77; in SMSA/non-SMSA, 80; in rural areas, 99–100; in towns and small cities, 106–07; in urbanized areas, 112–13